Miss Pe
Match Making Club
By Morgan Steele

This is a work of fiction. Similarities to real people, places, or events are entirely coincidental.

MISS PEARL'S MATCH MAKING CLUB

First edition. October 30, 2024.

Copyright © 2024 Morgan Steele.

ISBN: 979-8227253019

Written by Morgan Steele.

Also by Morgan Steele

Magnolia Springs
Miss Pearl's Match Making Club

Misfit Tour Guide Series
Adventures of a Misfit Tour Guide
Adventures of a Misfit Safari Guide

Montana Cowboys
Montana Cowboy
Rescue of the Heart

Shadows of Corruption
Shadows of Treason
Whispers in the Shadows

Whiskey Creek Cowboys
Cowboys of Whiskey Creek "Jake"

Standalone
Mishaps, a Cat and Love

Table of Contents

Chapter 1 1
Chapter 2 6
Chapter 3 15
Chapter 4 29
Chapter 5 34
Chapter 6 41
Chapter 7 52
Chapter 8 59
Chapter 9 67
Chapter 10 72
Chapter 11 81
Chapter 12 91
Chapter 13 95
Chapter 14 100
Chapter 15 107
Chapter 16 117
Chapter 17 125
Chapter 18 133
Chapter 19 142
Chapter 20 148
Chapter 21 153
Chapter 22 161
Chapter 23 170
Chapter 24 174
Chapter 25 182
Chapter 26 188
Chapter 27 193
Chapter 28 198
Chapter 29 202
Chapter 30 207

Chapter 1

Evie Matthews squinted as she stepped out of her old blue pickup truck, the kind that rattled as much as it drove. The sun was high, and the quaint town of Magnolia Springs, Georgia, population 6276, stretched out before her, as if it were a scene from a postcard. Quaint brick storefronts with painted signs, cozy cafes, and a town square dominated by an oversized magnolia tree filled the scene. Clara adjusted her sunhat, trying to get her bearings. The flower shop, her aunt's pride and joy, awaited just around the corner, ready for its new owner to breathe some life back into it.

As she walked down Main Street, she could feel the eyes of the townsfolk on her, watching her every move like hawks eyeing a stray chicken. They whispered and waved, offering hesitant smiles that made Evie feel like a curiosity rather than a new neighbor. A little girl in pigtails giggled, pointing at her, while her mother shushed her quickly. Evie forced a smile and waved back, feeling like she'd just landed in a small-town soap opera.

Evie stood on the front steps of Iris & Ivy, the flower shop she'd inherited from her late Aunt Iris. The old two story building was painted white and trimmed around the windows in ivy green and iris purple door which made the store front pop.

The morning sun cast a warm glow over Magnolia Springs, making the dew on the magnolia trees sparkle like tiny diamonds. The town square, just down the street, was already bustling with the hum of morning gossip, carried along by a breeze that held a hint of the end of summer. The oversized magnolia tree in the center of the square towered like a sentinel, its wide branches stretching out protectively over the park benches and gazebo.

She hadn't been in Magnolia Springs, Georgia for years. The last time had been before her parents had been killed by a drunk driver almost ten years ago. Her aunt's passing last month was totally unexpected and had left Evie with a whirlwind of emotions and responsibilities, not the least of which was keeping the flower shop afloat. Evie had grown up spending every summer with her aunt, being taught the art of floral arranging. But the most important things she learned from her aunt was all the town quirks and the local's propensity for spreading gossip. But living here full-time would be a different experience altogether.

She opened the purple shop door, a small brass bell tinkling cheerily, and stepped inside. The flower shop smelled of a mixed floral scents and eucalyptus, a comforting mix that reminded Evie of lazy afternoons spent with Aunt Iris. The shop had retained its cozy charm, wooden shelves lined with vases, the little wicker baskets filled with dried lavender, and a countertop with an ancient cash register that creaked with every sale. On the front of the wooden counter just below the old register hung a round wooden plaque. The plaque was large and was painted white, with a large purple irises in the center surround by a ivy border. It was as if Iris was still there, her presence lingering in the soft corners of the room.

She glanced at the clock. It was barely 8 AM. Early for customers, even in a town like Magnolia Springs.

The bell above the door jingled and, Evie's eyes met those of Miss Pearl, the town's self-appointed matchmaker and gossip queen. The older woman, dressed in her usual floral print dress with pearls around her neck, leaned casually against the doorway, her silver hair pinned into an elegant twist. Her bright blue eyes twinkled with a mix of curiosity and mischief.

"Morning, Evie, dear," Miss Pearl drawled, her southern accent as thick as honey. "I thought I'd stop by before my morning tea with the girls and see if you have started to settle in."

Evie smiled politely, tucking a loose strand of auburn hair behind her ear. "Morning, Miss Pearl. I'm just about to start on that. Was there something you needed?"

Miss Pearl waved a hand dismissively, stepping further into the shop and casting a critical eye around. "I came to check on you. It's not easy for a young woman like yourself to deal with all this." She said waving her hands around.

Evie sensed the underlying intent behind the words. Miss Pearl rarely did anything without an ulterior motive. She straightened her shoulders, forcing a cheerful note into her voice. "I'm managing just fine, thank you. Aunt Iris taught me everything I need to know."

Miss Pearl's lips curved into a knowing smile. "I'm sure she did, bless her heart. But Magnolia Springs can be a little... lonely, don't you think? A young lady like yourself shouldn't be cooped up in a flower shop all day. You need to get out, meet new people. Maybe a nice, dependable man who could help with some of those heavier deliveries."

Evie stifled a sigh, recognizing this particular tune. "I appreciate the thought, but I'm really focused on the shop right now. Plus, I already know plenty of folks around here already."

Miss Pearl raised an eyebrow, her smile widening. "Oh, I know, I know. But most of them are hardly your age, now are they? Or single, for that matter. I was just talking to Ruby from the diner this morning, and she was saying how much she missed seeing fresh faces around here. Of course, she wasn't talking about you specifically, but... well, you know how it is."

Evie bit back a laugh, knowing all too well how the gossip wheel spun in Magnolia Springs. Everyone knew everyone's business, and they rarely hesitated to offer unsolicited advice. But despite herself, she found it hard to be annoyed with Miss Pearl. The woman had a genuine warmth behind her meddling, like an overenthusiastic grandmother who just wanted to see everyone settled and happy.

"Well, you know where to find me if you need anything," Miss Pearl said, patting Evie's arm with a surprisingly strong grip. "And don't worry, dear, I'm sure good things are just around the corner for you. You never know what might happen."

Evie managed a smile, even as she wondered what scheme Miss Pearl might be brewing. "Thanks, Miss Pearl. I'll keep that in mind."

Miss Pearl gave her a wink and headed for the door, but not before pausing dramatically on the threshold. "Oh, and by the way, I hear we might have a new addition to the town. A gentleman, if you catch my meaning." She left without another word, the bell above the door ringing as it closed behind her.

Evie stared at the door for a moment, then shook her head with a bemused smile. Miss Pearl and her cryptic comments, who knew what that woman was planning? She turned back to her work, trying to ignore the faint flutter of curiosity in her chest. Magnolia Springs had a way of pulling you into its orbit, and it seemed she was already caught up in its gravity.

Over the next few hours she had more visitors. Each one brought a bit of news or gossip, like a puzzle piece of the town's daily life. She learned that Daisy one of the librarian was planning a new history exhibit at the library that Ruby's diner was hosting a pie-eating contest for the upcoming Harvest Festival in a few months, and that Earl was still struggling to fix the old barber chair that had been squeaking for weeks.

By the time lunchtime rolled around, Evie had a flower order placed and found herself smiling more easily. There was something comforting about the steady rhythm of life in Magnolia Springs, even if it meant being the subject of idle chatter. She paused to eat her sandwich behind the counter, glancing out the window toward the business next door. She was told the shop had been closed for a few months, ever since old man Mr. Bennett and his wife had retired and moved to Florida. It was strange to think that someone new might be moving in, another change in a year that had already been full of them.

Evie took a sip of sweet tea, letting her mind wander. Maybe a new neighbor wouldn't be such a bad thing, she mused. It might bring a little more foot traffic to her shop. And who knew? Maybe Miss Pearl's mysterious "gentleman" wouldn't be half as meddlesome as she imagined.

But just as she allowed herself that small hope, the lights in the back room flickered. She froze, her sandwich halfway to her mouth. The air around her seemed to grow colder, and she felt a faint brush of something like a whisper against her ear. Evie quickly set down her lunch, her heart racing as she scanned the room for any logical explanation.

Nothing. The room was empty except for the flowers and vases.

She let out a shaky breath, forcing herself to relax. "It's just the wiring," she muttered to herself. "This building is older than dirt. It's probably nothing."

But as she turned to pick up her sandwich again, she couldn't shake the feeling that maybe, just maybe, there was something more to Iris & Ivy than she'd originally thought. Something that might take more than flowers and good intentions to handle.

Chapter 2

Grayson Bennett parked his pickup truck in front of Bennett's Tools & Fix-It, the hardware store he was reopening. He climbed out, his boots crunching against the gravel as he glanced at the freshly painted sign swinging gently above the storefront. Magnolia Springs hadn't changed much in the years he'd been gone, same familiar streets, same gossipy residents, and the same charmingly nosy atmosphere that he'd tried to escape when he left for college.

But after nearly a decade of working in construction in Atlanta, he'd found himself missing the slow, steady rhythm of his small hometown life. He had made really good money over the past decade, enough to buy the hardware store and run it for quite a while, but there are somethings money can't buy, like slow pace tranquility. Even though Atlanta was only a few hundred miles away, it felt like a million compared to Magnolia Springs. .His uncle's retirement offered the perfect excuse to come back home, take over the family business, and maybe, just maybe, find a sense of peace he hadn't realized he'd been looking for.

Grayson gave the door a shove, and it swung open with a satisfying creak. Inside, the shop smelled faintly of sawdust and oil, just as he remembered it. He surveyed the space, rows of shelves stocked with nails, screws, paint cans, and tools lined up like soldiers ready for duty. He made a mental note to order some new inventory and spruce up the place a bit, but overall, it had the same comfortable, worn-in feel he'd grown up with.

Grayson glanced up at the ceiling and smiled as he thought of the large 3 bedroom residence upstairs. No house hunting for him. It was in need of serious updating, but nothing he couldn't handle.

He was halfway through arranging a display of new hammers when the sound of footsteps echoed outside. He glanced through the dusty window just in time to see Miss Pearl making a beeline for his shop, a determined look on her face. Grayson stifled a groan. He'd barely been back in town for a week, and already, Magnolia Springs' resident matchmaker had him in her sights.

"Grayson Bennett!" she called, her voice carrying through the open door before she even stepped inside. "I thought I saw your truck out here. It's about time you showed your face around town again!"

Grayson set down the hammer he'd been holding and turned to face her with a polite smile. "Morning, Miss Pearl. You're up and about early."

Miss Pearl swept inside like she owned the place, which, in a way, she practically did, at least in spirit. She looked him up and down, her sharp blue eyes missing nothing. "Well, I had to see if the rumors were true. Imagine my surprise when I heard that handsome young Grayson Bennett was back in town to take over the old hardware store."

Grayson chuckled, running a hand through his tousled dark brown hair. "You know me, Miss Pearl, couldn't stay away forever. Figured it was time to come back and settle down."

Her smile widened at his choice of words, and Grayson immediately regretted giving her any encouragement. "Settle down, hmm? Well, isn't that just interesting! Magnolia Springs could use more eligible young men like you around. It's been far too quiet since Earl's nephew moved away last year."

Grayson leaned against the counter, crossing his arms. "Somehow, I doubt the town's been all that quiet."

"Oh, you'd be surprised, dear." She paused, glancing out the window toward the flower shop next door, Evie's shop. "Speaking of which, have you met your new neighbor yet? Miss Evie Matthews, runs Iris & Ivy. She's a sweet girl, but bless her heart, she's got her hands full with that old building."

Grayson followed her gaze, curiosity stirring. He'd noticed the flower shop in passing, with its neat display of potted plants and the cheerful "Open" sign in the window. But he hadn't yet introduced himself to the new owner. "Can't say I have, but I'm sure we'll cross paths eventually."

"Oh, I'm sure you will," Miss Pearl said, a hint of mischief in her tone that set off warning bells in Grayson's head. "That building of hers has seen better days. Drafty, you know. And those old buildings, well, sometimes they have a mind of their own. I do hope she doesn't get too spooked over there all by herself."

Grayson narrowed his eyes slightly, trying to read the look on her face. "Is that right? I thought it seemed like a nice place."

Miss Pearl waved a hand airily. "Oh, it is! But you know how these things go... an old building, some creaky floorboards. A young woman alone. It wouldn't hurt for a nice, capable neighbor like yourself to keep an eye out, hmm?"

Grayson suppressed a smile. "I'll keep that in mind, Miss Pearl. Thanks for the heads up."

She beamed at him, clearly pleased with herself. "Well, I'll let you get back to your work, dear. But don't be a stranger, now. We're all so excited to have you back in Magnolia Springs."

With that, she swept out the door, leaving behind the faint scent of lavender and a lingering sense that she'd set some sort of plan into motion. Grayson watched her go, shaking his head in amusement. Miss Pearl hadn't changed a bit, in fact she seems to have become more mischievous.

He spent the rest of the morning tidying up the store, but his thoughts kept drifting back to the flower shop next door. What kind of woman was Evie Matthews? He pictured a sweet, shy florist, probably not much interested in gossip or meddling neighbors. He couldn't imagine her wanting to get caught up in whatever schemes Miss Pearl had in mind.

By the time noon rolled around, he decided to take a break and grab some lunch from Ruby's Diner across the square. He locked up the shop and stepped outside, only to hear a crash from next door. He paused, listening. A moment later, he heard a muffled curse and the clatter of something hitting the floor. It sounded like trouble.

Without thinking, Grayson crossed the short distance between their storefronts and rapped on the glass door of Iris & Ivy. "Everything all right in there?"

The door swung open before he finished speaking, revealing a flustered-looking woman with auburn hair pulled into a messy bun and green eyes that sparkled with frustration. She was petite but carried herself with a kind of stubborn determination that Grayson found oddly charming.

"Sorry about that," she said, brushing a strand of hair out of her face with a sheepish smile. "Just had a little... vase mishap."

Grayson glanced past her into the shop, where a pile of ceramic shards lay scattered on the floor amidst a bunch of spilled stems of irises. He couldn't help but chuckle. "Looks like more than a little mishap. Need a hand?"

She hesitated, clearly torn between accepting the offer and maintaining her pride. After a moment, she sighed and stepped back. "If you don't mind. I don't know what happened, one minute it was sitting on the shelf, not even close to the edge and the next I watched it tip over and fall. It was empty and not even close to the edge, I swear."

"Don't worry, I've seen worse," he assured her, stepping inside. The shop was filled with a warm, earthy scent, and despite the mess, it had a cozy, inviting atmosphere. He knelt down to help her pick up the pieces, noticing the way her cheeks flushed slightly pink as she worked.

"I'm Evie, by the way. Evie Matthews. I run the flower shop... obviously," she said with a nervous laugh.

"Grayson Bennett," he replied, offering her a small smile. "I Just moved back to town to take over the hardware store next door."

Evie glanced up at him, curiosity flickering in her eyes. "So you're the one Miss Pearl's been talking about. She's been saying the town could use a few more eligible bachelors."

Grayson rolled his eyes good-naturedly. "Sounds about right. She already stopped by this morning to 'welcome me back.' She's got quite a talent for knowing everyone's business."

Evie snorted softly. "Yeah, you'll get used to it. She's harmless, but she's definitely got a knack for matchmaking, or so I've been told."

They worked together in comfortable silence for a few minutes, gathering up the last of the shards and righting the flower display. Grayson couldn't help but notice the faint chill in the air, despite the warm sunshine streaming through the windows. He shivered slightly and glanced toward the back room, where shadows seemed to linger.

"Cold in here, isn't it?" he remarked casually, trying to gauge her reaction.

Evie bit her lip, a flicker of unease crossing her face before she forced a smile. "Yeah, the old building's got some quirks. I think there's a draft in the back room or something. Aunt Iris always said this building had a mind of its own, but I think it's just the creaky floorboards."

Grayson chuckled, though he kept his tone light. "Well, if you ever need any help with the wiring or anything, just let me know. Wouldn't want you getting spooked."

Evie rolled her eyes, but there was a hint of a smile tugging at her lips. "Thanks, but I think I can handle a few flickering lights. Besides, I've got enough on my plate without worrying about ghosts."

Grayson nodded, but he made a mental note to keep an eye out anyway. There was something about the way she brushed off the suggestion that made him think she wasn't quite as unconcerned as she wanted to appear. He stood up, dusting off his hands. "Well, if you change your mind, or if you ever need anything, you know where to find me."

"I'll keep that in mind," she said, offering him a small, genuine smile. For a moment, they stood there, the air between them warm with unspoken possibilities. But then the bell above the shop door jingled, and Evie glanced past him to greet a new customer.

Grayson took that as his cue to leave, giving her a nod as he headed for the door. "Take care, Evie. And watch out for those rogue vases."

Evie laughed softly, shaking her head as she followed him to the door. "I'll do my best. Thanks for the help, Grayson."

He offered her a parting smile, then stepped back out onto the sidewalk. As the door closed behind him, he couldn't help but glance back through the window, catching one last glimpse of Evie returning to her work, a thoughtful expression on her face. There was something about her that he found intriguing, maybe it was the way she seemed both tough and vulnerable at the same time, or the way her laughter filled the quiet space of the flower shop. Whatever it was, he had a feeling he'd be seeing more of her.

He shook off the thought as he made his way across the square to Ruby's Diner, the familiar buzz of small-town life greeting him like an old friend. The diner was a cozy little spot with checkered floors and red vinyl booths that had seen better days. Ruby, the owner, stood behind the counter, flipping through a menu with the focus of a scientist, her graying hair pinned up in a messy bun.

"Well, if it isn't Grayson Bennett," she called out as he entered. "What brings you in today, handsome? Come to see if my food's as good as you remember?"

Grayson took a seat at the counter with a grin. "Figured I'd see if you're still burning the bacon, Ruby."

She rolled her eyes, but a smile tugged at the corners of her mouth. "You know darn well I never burn the bacon. Now, what'll it be? Got a special today, meatloaf with a side of gossip."

Grayson laughed and picked up the worn menu. "I'll take a burger, medium well, and skip the gossip, thanks."

Ruby snorted. "Good luck with that. The town's been buzzing ever since you came back. And don't think I haven't heard about Miss Pearl's little visit this morning. She's got plans for you, you know."

Grayson shook his head, but there was a bemused smile on his face. "Yeah, I got that impression. But I'm just here to run the hardware store, Ruby. Not looking for anything else."

Ruby shot him a knowing look as she poured him a glass of sweet tea. "You keep telling yourself that, honey. But I've been around long enough to know that when Miss Pearl sets her sights on something, she doesn't quit until she gets her way."

Grayson took a sip of the tea, savoring the familiar taste. "Well, she might have met her match this time."

Ruby just chuckled, looked at him like he was the stupidest man on the face of the earth, and went back to the grill, leaving Grayson to his thoughts. He couldn't deny that the prospect of getting caught up in Magnolia Springs' matchmaking schemes was less than appealing. But at the same time, he couldn't quite shake the memory of Evie's smile, or the way her green eyes had sparked with a mix of frustration and curiosity when they'd spoken.

As he waited for his burger, he glanced out the window, his gaze drifting back toward the flower shop across the square. Through the glass, he could see Evie arranging a new display of roses in the window, her movements quick and graceful despite the lingering tension in her shoulders. She seemed so focused, so determined to make a life for herself in this little town, even with all its quirks and challenges.

For a moment, he wondered what it would be like to be a part of that life, if only as a friend, someone she could count on when things got tough. He quickly pushed the thought away, reminding himself that he wasn't looking for complications. But still, as he turned back to his lunch, he couldn't quite shake the feeling that maybe, just maybe, coming back to Magnolia Springs might hold more surprises than he'd expected.

Back at Iris & Ivy, Evie tried to focus on her work and her customers, but her mind kept drifting back to Grayson Bennett. He was different from what she'd expected, easygoing and kind, with a smile that made her heart skip a beat if she was being honest with herself. And he hadn't seemed bothered by the odd chill in the shop or the strange noises that had been keeping her up at night.

She sighed, tucking a strand of hair behind her ear as she arranged the roses in a vase. Maybe Miss Pearl was right, and she really did need to get out more. But she wasn't ready to let someone like Grayson, or anyone, for that matter, into her carefully controlled world. Not when she was still trying to find her footing after Aunt Iris's death, and especially not when she still hadn't figured out what to make of the strange occurrences in the shop.

As if on cue, the lights flickered again, casting eerie shadows across the wooden floor. Evie froze, holding her breath as she listened for any other sounds. A faint creak echoed from the back room, followed by a whisper of cold air brushing against her cheek. She shivered, rubbing her arms to chase away the chill.

"Get a grip, Evie," she muttered to herself, setting the vase on the counter with a thud. "It's just an old building. Aunt Iris always said this place had a mind of its own."

But as she turned to head upstairs to her small apartment above the shop, she couldn't shake the uneasy feeling that maybe the whispers in the shadows weren't just in her imagination. She hurried up the creaky staircase, her footsteps echoing through the empty shop, and locked the door behind her.

Her apartment was small but cozy, with a sloping ceiling that made the whole space feel like a hidden attic. The walls were painted a soft, calming blue, and she'd filled the shelves with mementos from her travels, souvenirs she'd collected over the years, before she'd found herself back in Magnolia Springs. Photos of her and Aunt Iris lined the mantel, capturing moments of laughter and warmth that now felt like they belonged to another life.

Evie sank onto the couch, wrapping a worn quilt around her shoulders as she stared out the window at the town below. The square was peaceful in the evening light, and she could just make out Grayson returning to his shop across the street, a to-go bag from Ruby's Diner in hand, after picking up what must be his dinner. She watched as he disappeared through the front door, her thoughts drifting back to their encounter earlier.

Maybe Grayson was just another one of Miss Pearl's projects, but she couldn't help wondering what his story was. Why he'd come back to a town like Magnolia Springs when most people his age were eager to leave. She had her own reasons for staying, but she doubted they were the same as his.

With a sigh, she leaned back against the couch cushions, letting the quiet of the apartment settle around her. She had enough to worry about without getting tangled up in whatever schemes Miss Pearl had in mind. Tomorrow, she'd tackle the rest of her orders, maybe even take a look at the flickering lights herself. After all, she was capable of handling a few creaks and groans.

But as she drifted off that night into a restless sleep, the faint sound of whispers seemed to echo through the shop below, weaving through her dreams like a thread of cold air. And somewhere in the back of her mind, she wondered if Grayson Bennett might just be the kind of trouble she didn't know she needed.

Chapter 3

Evie woke up to the soft sound of birds chirping outside her window, the morning sun streaming in through the thin curtains of her apartment above Iris & Ivy. She stretched, trying to shake off the lingering unease from the strange whispers that had haunted her dreams. As she got ready for the day, she tried to focus on the tasks ahead, filling orders, restocking inventory, and, hopefully, finding a way to fix the mysterious drafts in the shop.

She made her way downstairs, the familiar scent of flowers enveloping her as she unlocked the shop door and flipped the "Closed" sign to "Open." She'd just finished setting out a new display of sunflowers when the bell above the door jingled, and a cheerful voice called out, "Morning, Evie! I brought us coffee!"

Evie turned with a smile as Clara Wright, her best friend from her childhood visits and one of the few people in Magnolia Springs who knew her inside and out, bounded into the shop. Clara was all golden curls and infectious energy, with a wide smile that seemed to brighten every room she entered. Today, she wore a pair of faded jeans, a sunny yellow top, and a mischievous sparkle in her hazel eyes that always made Evie a little nervous.

"You're a lifesaver, Clara," Evie said, gratefully accepting the steaming cup of coffee. She took a sip and sighed in contentment. "I swear, you're the only thing keeping me from running out of this town some days."

Clara laughed, leaning against the counter with a wink. "Oh, don't say that! You know you love it here, creepy noises and all. Besides, where else would you find friends like me?"

Evie rolled her eyes but couldn't help smiling. "True, but you have to admit, this old building has a mind of its own. I don't know how Aunt Iris put up with all the strange drafts and flickering lights for so many years."

Clara's smile softened, a touch of sympathy in her eyes. "Your aunt had a way of seeing the good in things, you know? She probably thought it added character."

"Or she was just too stubborn to admit it was creepy," Evie joked, though her smile faltered slightly. She missed her aunt more than she liked to admit, especially on mornings like this, when the shop felt too big and empty.

Clara nudged her playfully, pulling her out of her thoughts. "Well, you've got me, and you've got the whole town wrapped around your little finger. Seriously, Evie, people adore you. And if you ever need a hand, you know I'm just a call away."

Evie shot her a grateful look. "Thanks, Clara. I appreciate it. And I might take you up on that offer if the wiring keeps acting up. Grayson Bennett help me cleaning up mess yesterday. It was the strangest thing a pottery vase jumped off the shelf and knocked over a container of Irises"

Clara's eyes widened, and a sly smile spread across her face. "Oh, really? Your *handsome* new neighbor next door? Now that's interesting."

Evie groaned, recognizing the gleam in Clara's eyes all too well. "Don't you start too, Clara. It wasn't anything like that. He was just being neighborly."

"Oh, I'm sure he was," Clara said, her tone dripping with mock innocence. "But don't you think it's a little bit of fate, him showing up right when you need a hand? Magnolia Springs does have a way of bringing people together, you know."

Evie gave her a skeptical look. "You sound just like Miss Pearl."

Clara's grin widened, but she quickly took another sip of her coffee to hide it. "Well, you know what they say, great minds think alike."

Evie arched an eyebrow, her suspicion growing. "Clara, please tell me you're not in on whatever scheme Miss Pearl's cooking up. I can handle her meddling, but if you start getting involved..."

Clara waved a hand dismissively, though her smile remained firmly in place. "Relax, Evie. I'm just saying that maybe the universe is giving you a little nudge. And if it happens to come with a side of Miss Pearl's matchmaking, well, what's the harm in that?"

Evie crossed her arms, but there was no real heat behind the gesture. She knew Clara meant well, and despite her exasperation, she couldn't deny that a small part of her was flattered by the attention. "Just promise me you won't go overboard, okay? I've got enough on my plate without worrying about surprise blind dates or 'accidental' run-ins."

Clara raised her hand solemnly. "Scout's honor. No surprise blind dates. But I reserve the right to hope for a little romantic magic."

Evie laughed despite herself, and Clara joined in, the sound of their laughter filling the shop and chasing away the lingering shadows from the night before. For a moment, everything felt light and easy, just like old times.

But then the bell above the door jingled again, and the warm atmosphere shifted as Miss Pearl herself swept into the shop, her bright eyes immediately zeroing in on the two friends. She was dressed in a prim lavender cardigan and a pearl necklace that looked as if it had been passed down for generations, and she carried an air of purpose that made Evie's stomach sink.

"Good morning, girls!" Miss Pearl said, her voice syrupy sweet. "I hope I'm not interrupting anything important."

Clara shot Evie a quick, conspiratorial look before turning to Miss Pearl with her most innocent smile. "Oh, not at all, Miss Pearl. Just catching up over coffee. What brings you in today?"

Miss Pearl clasped her hands together, her gaze darting between Clara and Evie with a knowing twinkle. "Well, I thought I'd stop by and see if Evie needed any help with those pesky drafts. You know, this building's been giving folks trouble for as long as I can remember. And it never hurts to have a little extra support, especially when there's a handsome new neighbor willing to lend a hand."

Evie resisted the urge to groan, glancing at Clara, who was doing a terrible job of hiding her smirk behind her coffee cup. "Thank you, Miss Pearl, but I think I've got it under control. Besides, I wouldn't want to impose on Grayson."

"Oh, nonsense," Miss Pearl said, waving a dismissive hand. "That's what neighbors are for, dear. And he's already settled back in to our little town. Why, I think he's just what our little community has been needing."

Clara's smile widened, and she nodded enthusiastically. "She's right, Evie. I went to school with Grayson, even though he's a few years older than me, he was always a nice guy. And it wouldn't hurt to have a little help, would it?"

Evie shot her friend a look, but Clara just shrugged innocently. It was clear that she and Miss Pearl were on the same page, even if Evie was still skeptical of their intentions. But before she could protest further, Miss Pearl stepped closer, lowering her voice to a conspiratorial whisper.

"You know, dear, I always say that a little mystery adds spice to life. And there's something about this old building of yours that's just begging for a story. Why, I wouldn't be surprised if there were a few secrets left behind by your Aunt Iris herself. A ghost, perhaps?"

Evie rolled her eyes, though she couldn't deny the shiver that ran down her spine at the mention of her aunt. "I'm sure it's just the drafts, Miss Pearl. Nothing supernatural."

Miss Pearl chuckled, but her expression turned more serious as she reached out to pat Evie's arm. "Well, if you ever need anything, you know where to find me. And don't be afraid to lean on those around you, dear. That's what this town is for."

Evie managed a smile, touched despite her frustration. "Thanks, Miss Pearl. I'll keep that in mind."

With a satisfied nod, Miss Pearl turned and made her way back toward the door, but not before shooting Clara a pointed look that made it clear their alliance was far from over. Clara gave her a discreet thumbs-up, which Evie pretended not to see.

As the door closed behind Miss Pearl, Evie let out a sigh and turned to Clara, raising an eyebrow. "So, care to explain what that was all about?"

Clara grinned, unrepentant. "Come on, Evie, you know she means well. And honestly, I think you could use a little excitement in your life. Besides, don't you think there's a certain charm to the idea of a haunted flower shop?"

Evie shook her head, but she couldn't help the small smile that tugged at her lips. "You're incorrigible, you know that?"

Clara leaned closer, her voice dropping to a playful whisper. "And you love me for it."

Evie couldn't argue with that. Despite the meddling and the schemes, she knew Clara had her back, just like she always had. And maybe, just maybe, there was a part of her that didn't entirely mind the idea of a little mystery, or the thought of getting to know her new neighbor a bit better.

Evie couldn't shake the feeling that she was standing on the edge of something she couldn't quite define, something that might change her life in ways she wasn't sure she was ready for. And somewhere in the shadows of Iris & Ivy, a whisper seemed to echo her thoughts, trailing through the quiet corners of the shop like a gentle breeze.

As the morning passed, Evie tried to focus on her work, rearranging displays and tidying up the shelves. But every now and then, she would catch herself glancing toward the back room, where the shadows seemed to linger a little longer than they should. She told herself it was just her imagination that she was letting Miss Pearl's stories get to her.

Still, as the afternoon sunlight began to slant through the front windows, painting the shop in warm golden hues, Evie found herself growing more restless. She decided to tackle some of the clutter in the back room, hoping that a bit of physical work would help clear her mind. She set down her pruning shears and headed to the back, where stacks of old boxes and dusty flowerpots lined the shelves.

She was halfway through sorting a box of vintage vases when a sudden chill swept through the room, raising the hairs on the back of her neck. Evie froze, listening as a faint creak echoed from above. Her apartment was empty, she knew that much, but the sound sent a shiver racing down her spine.

She took a deep breath, trying to steady her nerves. "It's just an old building," she muttered to herself. "Just the wind."

But the words did little to calm her racing heart. The shadows in the corner seemed to shift slightly, as if something, or someone, was moving just out of sight. Evie swallowed hard, telling herself she was being ridiculous. She turned back to the box, but her hands were shaking, and the vases clinked together as she tried to set them down.

Before she could talk herself out of it, she grabbed her phone and dialed Clara's number, her fingers fumbling slightly as she hit the call button. It rang twice before Clara's cheerful voice answered. "Hey, Evie! What's up?"

Evie forced a laugh, trying to keep her tone casual. "Hey, Clara. You wouldn't, uh, happen to be in the neighborhood, would you?"

Clara's voice took on a teasing lilt. "Are you calling because you miss me already, or because you're spooked by the ghost stories?"

Evie huffed out a breath, glancing warily at the shadows. "A little of both, maybe. I just thought, you know, if you weren't too busy, you could swing by and help me with some of these boxes."

Clara laughed softly. "All right, I'm on my way. Just promise you won't run off with the ghost before I get there."

Evie managed a small smile, her nerves easing just a bit at the sound of her friend's voice. "No promises. Thanks, Clara."

She hung up and set her phone on the counter, trying to focus on the task at hand while she waited. But her mind kept wandering back to the strange noises and flickering lights. She wondered if Aunt Iris had ever mentioned anything about the shop being haunted, but all she could remember were her aunt's lighthearted jokes about the building's quirks.

A soft knock on the front door made her jump, and she nearly dropped the vase she was holding. She turned quickly, relief washing over her when she saw Clara's smiling face peering through the glass. Evie hurried to the door, and pulling it open.

"You made good time," Evie said, trying to sound nonchalant as she stepped aside to let Clara in.

Clara grinned as she slipped through the doorway, her eyes twinkling with amusement. "Well, I couldn't let my best friend be haunted all by herself, could I?"

Evie rolled her eyes but couldn't help smiling. "Very funny. Come on, I could use an extra pair of hands with these boxes."

Clara followed her to the back room, glancing around with open curiosity. "So, what's the latest ghostly incident? Flickering lights, weird noises, or did the flowers start arranging themselves?"

Evie sighed, rubbing her arms as the cool draft returned. "Just the usual weird noises and cold spots. But it feels... different, somehow. Like there's something just out of sight."

Clara's expression softened, and she rested a reassuring hand on Evie's shoulder. "Hey, it's probably just the wind, like you said. Old buildings do that sometimes. But if it makes you feel better, I'll hang around until you're ready to close up for the day."

Evie shot her a grateful look. "Thanks, Clara. You know I don't really believe in ghosts, but... it's nice to have someone here."

Clara winked. "Well, I am off work today from the bank, so I'm happy to play ghostbuster for you, as long as you promise not to let this spook you out of town. Magnolia Springs wouldn't be the same without you."

They set to work unpacking boxes and tidying up the back room, the familiar rhythm of Clara's chatter helping to distract Evie from her unease. But as they worked, a soft creak sounded from above, followed by the unmistakable sound of footsteps crossing the ceiling.

Both women froze, their eyes meeting in the dim light of the back room.

"Okay, that one wasn't me," Clara said, her voice barely above a whisper. She glanced toward the staircase leading to Evie's apartment. "Did you leave a window open up there?"

Evie shook her head, her heart pounding in her chest. "No... no, I made sure everything was closed this morning."

Clara straightened, a determined look on her face. "Well, there's only one way to find out what's going on. Come on, let's go check it out."

Evie hesitated, but Clara grabbed her hand, pulling her toward the stairs before she could protest. They crept up the narrow staircase, the wood groaning softly beneath their feet, until they reached the door to Evie's apartment. Evie held her breath as she turned the knob, easing the door open.

The apartment was exactly as she'd left it, cozy, quiet, and perfectly undisturbed. The slanted sunlight cast long shadows across the floor, but there was no sign of any intruder. Evie let out a shaky laugh, feeling a bit foolish for letting herself get so worked up.

"See?" Clara said, releasing her hand with a triumphant grin. "Nothing to worry about. Probably just the wind rattling the roof or something."

Evie managed a sheepish smile. "Yeah, you're right. I'm just letting my imagination get the better of me."

Clara clapped her hands together. "Exactly! Now, how about we head back downstairs, finish those boxes, and then I'll treat you to a slice of pie at Ruby's? My treat."

Evie nodded, feeling her nerves start to settle. "That sounds great, actually. Thanks, Clara. I don't know what I'd do without you."

Clara's smile softened, and she pulled Evie into a quick, tight hug. "You'll never have to find out, because I'm not going anywhere."

They headed back downstairs, the shadows in the shop seeming a little less ominous with Clara's reassuring presence by her side. Evie still wasn't sure what to make of the strange occurrences in the building, but she felt a little more prepared to face them, especially knowing she had a friend like Clara watching her back.

As they reached the bottom of the stairs, the bell above the shop door jingled again, and Evie looked up to see Grayson Bennett stepping inside, a curious look on his face. He glanced between the two women, then raised an eyebrow.

"Everything okay in here?" he asked, his deep voice filling the small space. "I thought I thought I saw someone walking around in your upstairs window."

Clara shot Evie a meaningful look, but Evie ignored her, offering Grayson a polite smile. "Everything's fine, it was just us walking around because we thought we heard someone up there walking around. Thanks for checking in, though."

Grayson nodded, but his gaze lingered on Evie, as if he could see right through her calm facade. "Well, if you ever need help, you know where to find me. I've dealt with plenty of old buildings in my time."

Clara nudged Evie with her elbow, but Evie shot her a warning look before turning back to Grayson. "Thanks, Grayson. I appreciate it. I'm sure we'll be fine."

Grayson's lips twitched with the hint of a smile, and he nodded toward the back room. "Mind if I take a look around? I know you're not keen on outside help, but I've got a feeling your wiring might need more than just a quick fix."

Evie hesitated, but before she could answer, Clara piped up. "Oh, that's a great idea, Grayson! I'm sure Evie would be thrilled to have an expert's opinion."

Evie shot Clara a look that clearly said *traitor*, but Clara just smiled innocently. Grayson, meanwhile, seemed oblivious to the silent exchange, his attention focused on the darkened back room.

"All right," Evie said with a sigh. "If you really think it'll help, I suppose it couldn't hurt to have you take a look."

Grayson nodded, his expression turning serious as he stepped further into the shop. He headed toward the back room, his movements confident and assured, and Evie couldn't help but feel a flicker of admiration for the way he carried himself as he moved through the shop, taking in the details with a careful, practiced eye. He checked the old wiring along the walls, tested the creaky floorboards, and even peered up at the ceiling, where a few loose beams cast shifting shadows.

Clara watched him with barely contained amusement, nudging Evie again. "You see? He's practically a knight in shining armor, here to rescue you from the scary old building."

Evie shot her a warning glare, her cheeks warming despite herself. "Keep it up, Clara, and I'll make you restock the whole daisy display by yourself."

Grayson glanced back at the two of them, raising an eyebrow. "Am I missing something?"

"Oh, nothing at all!" Clara said, her smile widening as she winked at Evie. "Just talking about how grateful Evie is for your help."

Evie groaned inwardly but forced a polite smile. "I think what Clara means is that it's nice of you to check on things, Grayson. You really don't have to go to so much trouble."

Grayson shrugged, glancing back at the wiring. "No trouble at all. This place has a lot of charm, but I wouldn't be surprised if some of the electrical work is older than I am. Wouldn't want you getting hurt because of some faulty wiring."

Evie bit her lip, feeling a strange mix of gratitude and embarrassment. It wasn't often that someone offered her help without expecting anything in return, and she wasn't quite sure how to handle it. "Well... thank you. I'll try to be more careful."

Grayson finished his inspection and turned back to face her, his expression thoughtful. "If you like, I could come back this weekend and take a closer look. Maybe fix up some of these loose wires. Shouldn't take more than a few hours."

Evie opened her mouth to protest, but Clara cut in before she could speak. "That would be wonderful, wouldn't it, Evie? I'm sure you could use a little extra help, especially with all those wedding orders you've got coming up."

Evie shot Clara another glare but reluctantly nodded. "Okay, fine. If you're sure you don't mind, I'd appreciate the help."

Grayson smiled, a warm, genuine expression that softened the angles of his face. "Not at all. Just let me know when's a good time, and I'll bring my tools over."

Evie forced herself to smile back, even as her mind raced with the implications of spending more time with her new neighbor. She barely knew the man, but there was something about his steady presence that made her feel a little less alone in this old building with all its mysteries.

Clara, meanwhile, seemed entirely too pleased with herself. As Grayson wrapped up his inspection and made his way toward the door, she called after him, "Thanks again, Grayson! We'll make sure to keep the ghosts in check until you get back!"

Grayson chuckled as he turned back to face them. "Good luck with that. And try not to let Miss Pearl spook you too much, she's been telling ghost stories about this place for as long as I can remember."

Evie managed a laugh, but her mind lingered on the strange noises and whispers she'd heard. "I'll do my best. Thanks, Grayson."

With a final nod, Grayson stepped out into the sunlight, the bell above the door chiming softly as he left. Evie watched him go, a swirl of emotions she couldn't quite name tugging at her chest. She wasn't sure what to make of her new neighbor, or of the strange mix of relief and uncertainty she felt whenever he was around.

As soon as the door swung shut behind him, Clara let out a triumphant laugh and threw an arm around Evie's shoulders. "Well, well, look at that! He's practically smitten with you already. And you didn't even have to bat your eyelashes or anything."

Evie rolled her eyes, pushing Clara away with a playful shove. "You're ridiculous. He's just being nice, Clara. That doesn't mean he's interested."

Clara smirked, raising an eyebrow. "Oh, come on, Evie. A guy like that doesn't offer to fix your wiring just because he's feeling neighborly. Trust me, he's got his eye on you."

Evie shook her head, but she couldn't entirely dismiss the flicker of warmth that Clara's words sparked. "Even if that were true, which it's not, I don't have time for a relationship right now. I've got enough on my plate just keeping this shop running."

Clara sighed dramatically, but her expression softened as she glanced around the cozy, flower-filled space. "I know, Evie. But don't forget that it's okay to let people in sometimes. You don't have to carry everything on your own."

Evie felt a lump rise in her throat, and she swallowed hard, forcing herself to smile. "I'll keep that in mind. But for now, let's finish up those boxes before Miss Pearl comes back with another round of matchmaking plans."

Clara laughed, giving Evie's shoulder a squeeze. "Deal. But just so you know, I'm rooting for a little romance, ghosts or no ghosts."

They spent the next hour working side by side, unpacking boxes and restocking the shelves, the afternoon sunlight casting warm patterns across the floor. With Clara's cheerful presence filling the space, the shadows seemed to recede, and the chill that had haunted Evie earlier faded into the background.

But as the day drew to a close and Clara finally headed out with a promise to meet up again soon, Evie couldn't shake the feeling that something lingered in the quiet corners of Iris & Ivy, something that watched and waited, just out of sight.

She locked up the shop and made her way back up to her apartment, pausing at the top of the stairs to look out the window at the town below. Magnolia Springs was starting to settle into its evening routine, the last rays of sunlight painting the square in shades of gold and pink. Across the street, she could see Grayson closing up his hardware store, the shadow of his tall figure moving through the dim interior.

Evie leaned against the window frame, her thoughts drifting back to the unexpected encounters of the day. Maybe Clara was right, maybe it wouldn't be so bad to let herself hope for a little more than just running a flower shop in a sleepy town. But for now, she would take things one step at a time. She had enough mysteries to solve without adding romance to the list.

She turned away from the window and headed into her cozy kitchen. She decided to heating up some leftover fried chicken, mashed potatoes and a nice relaxing cup of tea. As she waited for the microwave to beep and the kettle to boil, she couldn't help but glance toward the shadows lurking in the corner of the room. She'd never been one to believe in ghosts, but tonight, she found herself whispering a quiet plea into the empty air.

"If you're out there, Aunt Iris... could you maybe give me a sign? Just to let me know I'm not going crazy?"

There was only silence for a heartbeat, but then the silence broken by the soft hiss of the kettle on the stove. Just as she turned away, the lights flickered again, once, twice, as if in answer. Evie froze, her heart skipping a beat as she stared at the bulb above her head.

She took a deep breath, forcing herself to smile. "Okay, then. I guess that's a yes."

She finished making her tea, grabbed her plate from the microwave and settled onto the couch with a blanket, letting the warmth of the cup soothe her frayed nerves.

She tried to get lost in her latest book she was reading, her mind kept drift to what the future may hold for her. Whatever the future held, be it ghosts, new neighbors, or Miss Pearl's schemes, she'd face it the same way she always had: with a steady heart and a stubborn determination to make her way.

After fighting to concentrate on the story, her eyes started to shut. Giving up on reading, she closed her book, and placed her plate and cup in the sink and made her way to her bedroom. She changed into her favorite camisole pajamas, brushed her teeth and crawled under the covers. As she drifted off to sleep, a faint breeze whispered through the room, carrying with it the scent of fresh flowers and the distant echo of laughter. Somewhere in the shadows, the past and the present mingled, weaving a story that had only just begun.

Chapter 4

Ruby's Café was buzzing with the morning crowd, the clatter of dishes and the hum of conversation filling the air. It was the kind of place where everyone knew your order before you walked through the door, and the coffee was as hot and strong as the gossip. Today, the back corner booth was occupied by a small group of women, all leaning in close, their voices hushed in a way that suggested serious business was being discussed.

At the center of this little assembly sat Miss Pearl, resplendent in her rose-patterned cardigan, her silver hair coiled neatly into a twist. On either side of her were her closest allies in the unofficial "Matchmaker Club" of Magnolia Springs, Betty, Ruby, and Hattie. Each woman wore an expression of intense focus, their eyes darting between the café entrance and the notebook Miss Pearl had spread open in front of her.

"I'm telling you, this is the perfect opportunity," Miss Pearl said, tapping the notebook with a manicured finger. "Evie's shop has just the right amount of old charm, and those quirks. Why, it's practically begging for a little... atmosphere."

Betty, who ran the town's hair salon, nodded eagerly, her bright red curls bobbing with enthusiasm. "And you know how skittish she is about all those noises in the building. I bet if we play this right, we could have her running straight into Grayson Bennett's arms."

Hattie, the town librarian, adjusted her glasses with a thoughtful frown. "But what if she catches on? Evie's sharp, and she might not appreciate us meddling in her business."

Miss Pearl waved a dismissive hand. "Oh, don't be such a worrywart, Hattie. She'll thank us in the long run. And besides, it's not like we're doing anything harmful, just adding a little... encouragement."

Ruby, who owned the café and was known for her no-nonsense attitude, leaned forward, her lips twitching with amusement. "You know, it's not a bad plan, Pearl. And I've got a few ideas of my own. I could rig up some of those old Halloween decorations we've got in storage, make them move around a bit, give her a good spook."

The group giggled, their laughter barely stifled as they leaned even closer over the table. They were so absorbed in their plotting that they almost didn't notice when the bell above the café door jingled, announcing a new arrival.

Evie Matthews stepped inside, blinking against the change in light as she looked around the bustling café. She had pulled her auburn hair into a loose ponytail, and she wore her usual uniform of jeans and a fitted t-shirt, practical and comfortable for a day of work. She had been so focused on running errands and thinking about the upcoming orders at Iris & Ivy that she almost missed the sudden silence that fell over the room.

She glanced over and found Miss Pearl, Betty, Ruby, and Hattie all staring at her with expressions that were far too innocent to be genuine. Their conversation cut off mid-sentence, and an awkward tension filled the air.

Evie forced a smile, her brow furrowing slightly as she took in the scene. "Morning, Miss Pearl, ladies," she said, her voice a little uncertain as she made her way to the counter. "Hope I'm not interrupting anything?"

Miss Pearl's smile widened, a little too quickly. "Oh, not at all, dear! We were just discussing... um, the plans for...um... the Harvest Festival in October. You know how it is, so much to organize."

Evie nodded slowly, but the nagging feeling that they were hiding something lingered. She turned toward Ruby who had walked behind the counter, placing her order for a turkey club sandwich and a sweet tea, but she couldn't shake the sensation that the group was watching her every move. When she glanced back over her shoulder, she found them whispering again, their heads bent together like a flock of conspiratorial hens.

Her cheeks flushed, and she quickly looked down at herself, checking for anything out of place. Was there something on her t-shirt? Had she spilled coffee on her jeans? She tugged at the hem of her t-shirt, smoothing out imaginary wrinkles, and adjusted the strap of her purse, trying to ignore the prickling feeling that they were talking about her.

Evie shifted awkwardly from one foot to the other as Ruby handed her the brown paper bag with her lunch. "Here you go, honey," Ruby said with a wink, clearly trying to hold back a smile. "Enjoy."

"Thanks, Ruby," Evie mumbled, still feeling the weight of the matchmakers' gaze. She turned to leave, offering the group a small wave. "I'll see you all later."

"Take care now, Evie!" Miss Pearl called after her, her tone a touch too cheerful. "And don't you worry about a thing. Everything's going to work out just fine, you'll see!"

Evie frowned, wondering what on earth that was supposed to mean. But she managed another smile and hurried out the door, the bell chiming behind her as she escaped into the fresh air of the town square. As she made her way back to Iris & Ivy, she couldn't help but glance over her shoulder, half-expecting to find the matchmakers still watching her through the window.

Once she was out of sight, Miss Pearl leaned back in the booth with a satisfied smile, tapping her pen against the notebook. "Well, that went just swimmingly. Now, where were we?"

Betty giggled, leaning forward eagerly. "We were talking about how to make sure she's properly spooked. I think Ruby's idea about the Halloween decorations is perfect."

Hattie adjusted her glasses, her brow furrowing with concern. "And you're sure this won't upset her too much? I mean, it's all in good fun, but I'd hate for her to think her shop is really haunted."

Miss Pearl patted Hattie's hand reassuringly. "Now, now, it's all part of the plan, Hattie. We're just giving her a little nudge. And besides, Grayson will be right next door to save the day. They'll bond over the experience, mark my words."

Ruby nodded, rubbing her hands together with a grin. "I'll dig out those old ghost props tonight. Should be easy enough to make them look convincing. We'll start with a few small things, then ramp it up if she doesn't take the bait."

Betty clapped her hands, her excitement bubbling over. "Oh, I just love a good love story! And those two would be so cute together. She's got that serious look about her, and he's got that rugged, man charm. It's like something out of a movie!"

Miss Pearl couldn't hide her own satisfaction as she closed her notebook with a decisive snap. "Exactly, Betty. And with a little help from us, they'll be sharing candlelit dinners before you know it. Now, here's the plan for tonight's setup..."

She leaned in, her voice lowering to a conspiratorial whisper as she outlined the finer details of their scheme. The other women listened intently, their eyes gleaming with anticipation as they imagined the scene unfolding.

By the time they finished, the café was beginning to empty out, and the sun had shifted higher in the sky. Miss Pearl gathered up her things, a pleased smile playing on her lips. "All right, ladies. We'll meet at the shop after dark, and we'll get everything in place. Let's give Evie and Grayson a haunting they won't forget."

They all stood, exchanging conspiratorial winks and hushed laughter as they made their way out of the café, each of them carrying a little piece of the plan. Magnolia Springs might have been a small town, but it was about to become the stage for their grandest matchmaking effort yet.

And as Miss Pearl stepped out onto the sidewalk, she couldn't help but feel a thrill of excitement at the thought of the coming days. Evie Matthews might not know it yet, but the winds of change, and a few carefully staged hauntings, were about to sweep through Iris & Ivy.

With a satisfied nod, she glanced up at the old magnolia tree swaying gently in the breeze. "Here's to love, laughter, and a little harmless mischief," she murmured under her breath, then headed off down the street, ready to put the first phase of their plan into action.

Chapter 5

Evie Matthews sat at her kitchen table, clutching a mug of chamomile tea with hands that wouldn't stop shaking. The events of the previous night had left her sleepless and on edge, and every creak or groan from the old building made her jump. She'd tried to convince herself that it was just her imagination, that there was nothing lurking in the shadows of Iris & Ivy, but she couldn't quite make herself believe it.

Now, that the sun had set outside her window, casting long shadows across the flower shop below, a knot of dread twisted in her stomach. She glanced at the clock, 9:15 p.m., and took a deep breath, telling herself she'd be fine. It was just one more night. She could handle it.

But as the minutes ticked by and darkness fell, the noises started again. First, there was a low creak from the back room, then a series of muffled thumps, like something heavy being dragged across the floor. Evie's heart leapt into her throat, and she wrapped her arms around herself, trying to ignore the chill creeping through the air.

She stood, trying to steel her nerves, but then came the scratching, long, deliberate scrapes that seemed to come from the Walls themselves or more specifically her hall closet. Evie swallowed hard, her breath coming in shallow gasps as she tiptoed toward the closet door to. She pressed her ear to the wood, listening as the sounds grew louder, closer, until she couldn't stand it anymore.

Something banged against the door, and Evie's resolve snapped. She bolted down the hall and out her apartment door, nearly breaking her neck on the stairs in her haste. With her heart pounding in her chest she launched herself out into the cold night air. She barely even registered the chill as she crossed the short distance to Grayson Bennett's next door, her slippers scuffing against the gravel as she hurried up to the back door that led to his upstairs apartment.

With her heart almost beating out of her chest, she banged frantically on the door, as she desperately tried to catch her breath. What felt like a life time, Grayson opened the door, his expression turning from surprise to concern in an instant. He was dressed in a pair of worn but comfortable looking sweat bottoms and a faded T-shirt, his dark hair rumpled as if he'd just gotten up from the couch.

"Evie? What's wrong?" he asked, stepping aside to let her in. "You look like you've seen a ghost."

She forced a shaky laugh, her voice wavering. "I think I have. Or at least, something's been making enough noise to wake the dead."

Grayson's brow furrowed, and he crossed his arms, his concern deepening. "What kind of noise? Is it the wiring again?"

Evie shook her head, wrapping her arms around herself. "No, it's worse this time, scratching, banging, like... like something's inside the walls. It's coming from the closet in the hallway upstairs. But I checked, and I can't figure out what it is. It doesn't sound like an animal."

Grayson's jaw tightened, and he grabbed a flashlight from the kitchen counter, gesturing for her to lead the way. "All right, let's go check it out. Stay close, and don't worry, I'm sure we'll figure out what's going on."

Evie nodded, her heart still racing as they made their way back to Iris & Ivy together. She felt a little less terrified with Grayson by her side, his steady presence grounding her. But as they stepped into the shop, the air seemed to grow colder, and the shadows seemed to stretch longer, like fingers reaching out from the darkness.

Grayson flicked on the flashlight, casting a beam of light across the rows of flowers, and Evie led him toward the staircase. As they climbed, the noises grew louder, a rhythmic thumping that seemed to echo through the walls. Evie clutched the banister, her nerves stretched taut, but she forced herself to keep moving.

When they reached the hallway, Evie pointed toward the closet door. "It's coming from in there. I swear, I don't know how, but—"

Grayson nodded, cutting her off with a reassuring squeeze of her shoulder. "It's okay. We'll take a look."

He opened the door to the two foot by four foot small space. He reached up and pulled the chain to the light in the center of the small room. It only contained a few small boxes and an old coat, the air musty with the scent of dust and mothballs. Grayson stepped inside, inspecting the walls with the flashlight, but just as Evie followed him into the closet, the door slammed shut behind her with a loud *bang*.

Evie yelped, spinning around to face the door. She grabbed the knob and tried to twist it desperately, but it wouldn't budge. "What—Grayson, the door, it's locked!"

Grayson turned, his own expression shifting from confusion to alarm as he tried the knob. "Hang on, it's jammed somehow. Let me see if I can—"

He pushed against the door with his shoulder, but it wouldn't give, as if some unseen force was holding it shut. Evie's breathe quickened, panic flaring in her chest as she pounded on the wood. "This door doesn't even have a lock! What is this happening?"

Grayson took a deep breath, forcing his voice to remain calm even as he strained against the door. "Its okay, Evie. We'll figure this out. It's probably just something caught in the frame, maybe a loose hinge. Just... try to stay calm."

Evie pressed her back against the wall, squeezing her eyes shut as she tried to steady her breathing. "Calm. Right. Easy for you to say."

Grayson let out a short, dry laugh, leaning back against the opposite wall of the cramped closet. "Hey, I'm stuck in here with you, remember? If we're trapped, we might as well make the best of it."

Evie managed a weak laugh, though her hands still trembled. "I guess I didn't plan on spending my night locked in a closet. You?"

Grayson shook his head, a small smile tugging at his lips despite the situation. "Not exactly. But if it's any consolation, I've been in weirder situations before."

Evie raised an eyebrow, curiosity momentarily distracting her from the panic clawing at her chest. "Oh, yeah? Like what?"

Grayson settled against the wall, the flashlight beam casting long shadows around them. "Well, let's see... There was the time I got stuck in a crawl space under a house while doing some renovations. The owner didn't realize I was down there and locked up for the weekend. I had to spend the night eating granola bars until someone came back."

Evie's eyes widened, a surprised laugh escaping her. "You're kidding. That sounds awful!"

Grayson shrugged, a sheepish grin on his face. "Yeah, it wasn't my finest moment. But I've learned to keep snacks in my truck just in case."

Evie couldn't help but smile, some of the tension easing from her shoulders. "I guess I'll have to add snacks to my emergency kit for the next time I get trapped in a closet by a ghost."

Grayson chuckled, his gaze softening as he looked at her. "You're handling this pretty well, all things considered."

Evie sighed, resting her head back against the closet wall. "I don't know if I'd say that. I just... I don't understand what's going on. First the noises, now this door, none of it makes any sense."

Grayson's expression turned more serious, and he reached out to squeeze her hand gently. "We'll figure it out, Evie. Whatever it is, you're not dealing with it alone."

Evie met his gaze, feeling a warmth spread through her chest that had nothing to do with fear. For a moment, the dimly lit, cramped closet felt almost cozy, and she realized that she didn't mind being stuck here as much as she might have expected. Grayson's presence made her feel... safe, in a way she hadn't felt since she'd inherited the shop.

They stood in silence for a while, listening to the distant creaks of the old building. The air felt strangely still, as if the house itself were holding its breath. But just as Evie was starting to think they might be stuck there all night, the closet door creaked, then swung open on its own, revealing the brightly lit hallway beyond.

Grayson shot to his feet, scanning the empty corridor. He glanced back at Evie, his brow furrowed with confusion. "Did you see that?"

Evie shook her head, staring at the open doorway with wide eyes. "No... and I'm not sure I want to know what just happened."

"I thought I saw..." Grayson started to say.

Evie's hand covered his mouth quickly. "Nope, don't want to know, Greyson."

Nodding, Grayson stepped out into the hallway, checking the area with a thoroughness that Evie found oddly comforting. He examined the closet door, the hinges, the frame, but found nothing that explained how it could have locked them inside. After a few more minutes of searching, he turned back to her with a resigned shrug.

"Nothing out of place, at least nothing I can see," he said. "But if anything else happens, you call me right away, okay?"

Evie nodded, hugging her arms around herself as she tried to steady her breathing. "Okay. Thanks, Grayson. I... I don't know what I'd do without you right now."

Grayson's expression softened, and he offered her a small, reassuring smile. "You don't have to thank me. I'll leave my cell number by the register. Just take care of yourself, Evie. And remember, you're not alone in this."

With that, he walked her back down the stairs, stopping write his number down on the note pad by the register and out through the front of Iris & Ivy, casting one last glance at the shadowy interior of the shop before stepping outside. The moonlight cast a silver glow over the town square, the air still carrying a chill from the night's strange events. Grayson turned back to Evie as they reached her front door, his expression serious but kind.

"If anything happens, you know where to find me," he said, resting a hand on the doorframe. "Don't hesitate, even if it's the middle of the night. And if you want, I can swing by in the morning and help you check things out again in daylight."

Evie managed a tired smile, her nerves still jangling but soothed by his steady presence. "I appreciate that, Grayson. Really, I do. I don't know if I'll sleep tonight, but... at least I know I'm not losing my mind."

Grayson chuckled softly, but his gaze was gentle as he met her eyes. "Hey, you're not the only one hearing strange things, so if you're crazy, then we both are. But I'm sure there's a perfectly logical explanation. Probably just a draft or something shifting in the walls."

Evie nodded, trying to convince herself that he was right. But as she watched him turn to leave, she couldn't help but glance back toward the shadows inside the shop, a shiver running down her spine. "Goodnight, Grayson. And... thanks again."

Grayson glanced back over his shoulder, offering her one last reassuring smile. "Goodnight, Evie. I'll see you in the morning."

With that, he disappeared into the darkness, his flashlight beam cutting through the shadows as he headed back toward his place next door. Evie watched him go, taking a deep breath before stepping back inside and closing the door behind her. She turned the lock with a sense of finality, as if trying to keep out whatever strange presence had haunted her shop.

She stood in the dimly lit entryway for a moment, listening to the creaks and groans of the old building, but the noises had quieted, leaving only the distant hum of the town at rest. It was almost as if whatever had been stirring the air had decided to call it a night.

With a tired sigh, Evie made her way back upstairs, trying to ignore the uneasy feeling that lingered in the back of her mind. She wrapped herself in a blanket and curled up on the couch, her thoughts drifting back to Grayson and the strange connection they'd shared in that dark, cramped closet.

It had been unexpected, the way they'd opened up to each other, sharing bits of their lives in the dim glow of the flashlight. And despite the fear and confusion that had led her to seek him out, Evie couldn't help but feel a flicker of something warmer beneath it all, a sense that maybe, just maybe, she wasn't as alone as she'd thought.

She closed her eyes, listening to the quiet murmur of the town outside her window, and for the first time in days, a small, tentative smile curved her lips.

As she drifted into a restless sleep, the thought lingered at the edge of her mind: maybe some hauntings weren't so bad after all.

Chapter 6

The morning sun was barely peeking over the rooftops of Magnolia Springs when Grayson Bennett made his way across the short distance to Iris & Ivy. The air was cool and crisp, with a hint of dew clinging to the grass, but the chill did little to deter his purpose. He had barely slept, his thoughts lingering on the strange night he'd spent locked in the closet with Evie and the odd occurrences in her flower shop.

As he reached the back door, he hesitated for a moment, glancing up at the windows of her apartment. He could see a faint shadow moving behind the curtains, and he raised his hand to knock, hoping she wouldn't mind the early visit.

The door opened before his knuckles could touch the wood, revealing a bleary-eyed Evie wrapped in a thick sweater, her hair pulled into a messy bun. Dark circles lingered beneath her eyes, but she managed a small, tired smile when she saw him.

"Morning, Grayson," she said, her voice a little hoarse from lack of sleep. "You're up early."

Grayson offered her a sympathetic look. "I figured I'd check in, make sure you're okay after last night. I know it was... a lot."

Evie nodded, stepping aside to let him in. "Yeah, that's putting it mildly. I feel like I've been through a war with my own house. Thanks for coming over."

Grayson walked into the shop, his eyes scanning the space out of habit, as if expecting to find some clue that would explain the strange noises. He turned back to her, his expression softening as he noticed how exhausted she looked. "How about this, let me buy you breakfast at Ruby's Diner. You could use a break, and I think we could both use some coffee."

Evie's smile grew a little less weary, and she tucked a stray strand of hair behind her ear. "That actually sounds really nice. Let me grab my purse, and we'll head over."

A few minutes later, they were walking side by side through the town square, the morning light casting a golden glow over the magnolia tree and the quaint storefronts. Magnolia Springs was waking up slowly, with shopkeepers flipping signs to "Open" and townsfolk stopping to chat on their way to work. Evie tried to shake off the lingering unease from the night before, focusing instead on the warmth of Grayson's presence beside her.

When they reached Ruby's Diner, Evie hesitated for a moment at the entrance, glancing through the window where she could see Miss Pearl and her friends gathered at their usual booth, deep in conversation. As soon as she opened the door, though, the chatter died down, and four pairs of eyes turned in their direction, watching with undisguised curiosity.

Evie felt her cheeks flush, and she leaned closer to Grayson as they made their way to a booth near the window. "Is it just me, or does it feel like they've been talking about me?" she whispered, her voice barely audible over the clinking of silverware and the murmur of other diners.

Grayson offered her a reassuring smile, though his gaze flicked briefly toward Miss Pearl's table. "Just ignore it, Evie. That's the way folks are around here, nosy, but mostly harmless. They probably just think it's interesting that we're having breakfast together."

Evie arched an eyebrow, shooting a skeptical look at the group of matchmakers. "Interesting, huh? Well, I wish they'd be a little less interested."

Grayson chuckled, his smile turning playful. "You'll get used to it. They've got hearts of gold, even if they can't keep their noses out of other people's business."

Evie managed a laugh, though she couldn't quite shake the feeling that there was more to the matchmakers' silence than idle curiosity. But she let it go, focusing instead on the comfort of sitting across from Grayson in the cozy warmth of the diner. They chatted about lighter things, Grayson's plans for the hardware store, the upcoming Harvest Festival, and the little quirks of life in Magnolia Springs.

For a little while, it almost felt normal, like they weren't dealing with mysterious hauntings or midnight disturbances. By the time they finished their breakfast, Evie felt a little more like herself, even if the memory of the past nights still lingered like a shadow in the back of her mind.

As they walked back to Iris & Ivy, the sun had climbed higher, warming the cool morning air. Grayson offered to help her with the shop's morning chores, but she waved him off with a smile, assuring him she could handle it. They lingered on the doorstep for a moment, an unspoken ease settling between them.

"Thanks for breakfast, Grayson," Evie said, glancing up at him with a smile. "I think I needed that."

Grayson smiled back, the corners of his eyes crinkling in that way that made him look even more ruggedly charming. "Anytime, Evie. And remember, if anything happens, no matter how small, just give me a call."

Evie nodded, her smile turning a little wry. "Will do. Though I'm hoping for a quiet night tonight."

Grayson chuckled softly. "We can always hope. bye, Evie."

"Bye, Grayson and thanks again."

They shared one last smile before he turned and walked back toward his place, the sound of his footsteps fading as he disappeared around the corner. Evie watched him go, feeling a warmth that had nothing to do with the sun on her face. She lingered on the doorstep for a moment, savoring the sense of peace that Grayson's company had brought.

But as soon as she stepped back inside and closed the door, the uneasy silence returned, wrapping around her like a cloak. She tried to focus on her work, arranging new deliveries, watering the plants, and preparing bouquets for the day, but the memory of the strange noises lingered at the back of her mind.

It was barely past dusk when the disturbances started again. This time, the scratching noises came from the side of the building, long, grating scrapes that seemed to vibrate through the walls. Evie froze in the middle of arranging a bouquet, her hands trembling as she listened to the eerie sounds. They were louder than before, more deliberate, as if something, or someone, was outside, trying to claw its way in.

Her heart pounded in her chest, and she grabbed her phone with shaking hands. She didn't even hesitate before dialing Grayson's number.

He picked up on the second ring, his voice steady and alert. "Evie? What's wrong?"

"It's the noises again," she said, her voice breaking with a mix of fear and frustration. "They're coming from outside this time, on the side of the building. I don't know what to do—"

"I'm on my way," Grayson said firmly. "Stay inside, and don't worry. I'll be there in a minute."

Evie clutched the phone, trying to focus on the sound of his voice as she waited. She peered out the window, straining to see through the shadows, but the street outside was empty, save for the faint glow of the lampposts. She couldn't see anything that could explain the scratching noises, and the thought of facing whatever was out there alone made her skin crawl.

A few minutes later, she heard the sound of footsteps approaching, and she ran to the back door, relief flooding through her when she saw Grayson jogging across the alley with a determined expression on his face.

But before he could reach the door, he stopped abruptly, his flashlight beam landing on a figure crouched by the side of the building, holding a long rake that scraped against the wooden siding. Evie blinked in disbelief as the light revealed the familiar face of Miss Pearl, her expression one of pure, unfiltered mischief.

Grayson let out a stunned laugh, shaking his head as he stepped closer. "Miss Pearl? What on earth are you doing out here?"

Miss Pearl straightened, brushing off her cardigan as if nothing was out of the ordinary. "Oh, well, I was just... um, doing a little late-night gardening. You know how those weeds can get if you don't stay on top of them."

Grayson raised an eyebrow, clearly trying to suppress his amusement. "With a rake? In the dark?"

Miss Pearl's cheeks flushed pink, but she managed to keep her composure, even as Evie stepped out onto the back porch, her eyes wide with disbelief. "Well, a lady's got to do what she's got to do," Miss Pearl said primly, though her smile wobbled at the edges.

Stepping out the back door, Evie glanced between Grayson and Miss Pearl, her confusion turning to a mix of frustration and bewilderment. "You've been the one making all those noises?" she asked, her voice rising.

Miss Pearl shifted on her feet, looking as sheepish as Evie had ever seen her. "Well, now, Evie, it was all in good fun! Just a little... encouragement, you know? To get you and Grayson talking."

Grayson let out a low sigh, running a hand through his hair as he glanced over at Evie. "I think you've got some explaining to do, Miss Pearl."

Evie crossed her arms, leveling a look at Miss Pearl that would have made most people wither. "Oh, you'd better start explaining," she said, her voice firm despite the tremor of laughter that threatened to break through. "Because right now, I'm wondering how many more surprises you've got up your sleeve."

Evie stared at Miss Pearl, the shock and disbelief still etched on her face as the realization sank in. Grayson stood beside her, his arms crossed, one brow raised as he waited for an explanation. Miss Pearl, meanwhile, shifted her weight from one foot to the other, clutching her rake like a schoolgirl caught sneaking out after curfew.

"Miss Pearl," Evie began, trying to keep her voice calm despite the mix of frustration and embarrassment bubbling up inside her, "are you telling me that all of those noises, the scratching, the bangs... all of that was *you*?"

Miss Pearl's smile faltered, but she lifted her chin with a touch of stubborn pride. "Well, not just me, dear. It was a group effort. Ruby, Betty, and Hattie helped too. We thought a few little bumps and scratches might encourage you to reach out for help, you see."

Evie's mouth fell open, her hands balling into fists at her sides. "You've been tormenting me with fake hauntings since I moved here? For weeks—"

Miss Pearl's brow furrowed, and she held up a hand, waving it back and forth in a flustered manner. "Oh, no, no, no, dear. Now that's not right. We've only been doing it since last night."

Evie blinked, her frustration giving way to confusion. "Last night? Miss Pearl, I've been hearing things for *weeks*. You've been at this for weeks."

Miss Pearl shook her head emphatically, her silver curls bouncing with the motion. "No, Evie, you must be mistaken. We didn't start our little... efforts until the night after you came into the café. That was the day we put our plan into action."

Evie felt a chill race down her spine, colder than the night air around them. She glanced at Grayson, whose expression had shifted from exasperation to something closer to concern. "You mean to tell me that the first night I was here, when I heard all those noises and the strange things that happened... that wasn't you?"

Miss Pearl's eyes widened, genuine surprise coloring her face. "Oh, no, dear. Whatever you heard before we started our plan, that wasn't us. We didn't even have our supply list ready until after you walked out of the café that day. I swear, Evie, whatever happened before that, well, it's a mystery to me too."

A silence fell over them, thick and heavy with unspoken questions. Evie's mind raced, trying to make sense of what she'd just heard. If Miss Pearl and her friends hadn't been behind the first night's noises, then what, or who, had been causing the disturbances?

Grayson reached out, resting a steadying hand on Evie's shoulder. "Hey, let's not jump to conclusions. Maybe there's a perfectly logical explanation we haven't figured out yet."

Evie nodded, but she couldn't ignore the uneasy feeling that curled in her chest. "Yeah... maybe," she said, though her voice lacked conviction. "But I have a feeling that whatever it is, it's not done with me yet."

Miss Pearl opened her mouth to speak, but for once, she seemed at a loss for words. The mischievous gleam in her eye had faded, replaced by a flicker of genuine concern as she glanced between Evie and Grayson.

"Well," Miss Pearl finally said, clearing her throat and tightening her grip on the rake, "I suppose we'll have to figure this out together. And... I might owe you an apology, Evie. We never meant to scare you so badly."

Evie managed a small, weary smile, though her mind was still buzzing with uncertainty. "It's okay, Miss Pearl. I appreciate the...

sentiment, I guess. But maybe next time, you could just try suggesting coffee instead of haunting my shop?"

Miss Pearl let out a nervous laugh, and even Grayson cracked a smile, though the tension between them hadn't fully eased. As they stood there in the cool night air, the distant sounds of Magnolia Springs settling down for the night, Evie couldn't help but feel that the mysteries of Iris & Ivy were far from over.

And somewhere in the shadows, just beyond the reach of the porch light, she thought she heard the faintest whisper of something that didn't quite belong.

Evie crossed her arms, taking a steadying breath as she stared at Miss Pearl, who still looked a bit sheepish holding the rake like it was her favorite gardening tool. But there was another question burning in the back of her mind, one that she couldn't ignore now that everything was spilling out in the open.

"There's one more thing, Miss Pearl," Evie said, her voice tight. She could feel Grayson's hand drop from her shoulder, and he shifted beside her, his attention fully on the conversation. "Last night, when Grayson and I got stuck in the closet upstairs... that was you too, wasn't it?"

Miss Pearl's expression turned puzzled, and she tilted her head to one side, as if Evie had just asked her to solve a riddle. "Stuck in a closet? Whatever do you mean, dear?"

Evie took a step forward, her frustration flaring again. "Don't play coy, Miss Pearl. Grayson and I were locked in the hallway closet for nearly an hour, and the door wouldn't open. It didn't even have a lock, but somehow it jammed shut on us. You expect me to believe that wasn't part of your little scheme?"

Miss Pearl's mouth fell open, and she took a step back, her hands clutching the rake as if it might anchor her to the earth. "Oh honey child, no. No, no, no," she stammered, her face flushing a deep shade of pink. "We would never go into your house and we sure didn't have anything to do with that. Why, I'd never dream of locking you in a closet! What if you'd gotten hurt?"

Evie's eyes widened, and a shiver ran down her spine. She turned to look at Grayson, who seemed just as stunned as she was. He opened his mouth to say something, but for once, even he seemed at a loss for words.

Miss Pearl continued to sputter, clearly flustered by the accusation. "We were just trying to give you both a little nudge, you know? With a few noises and bumps, but nothing dangerous! Locking a door? That's—that's something else entirely!"

Evie's mind whirled, the pieces of the puzzle scattering like petals in a strong wind. If Miss Pearl and her friends hadn't been behind the closet incident, then what, *or who*, had trapped her and Grayson inside?

She swallowed hard, trying to steady the pounding of her heart. "So you're telling me that while you and your friends were out here scratching at the walls, something else was going on inside the shop?"

Miss Pearl nodded vigorously, her curls bouncing as she clutched the rake even tighter. "Yes, dear, that's exactly what I'm saying! I promise you, we wouldn't do anything like that. The plan was just a little innocent mischief to get you and Grayson talking, not some... some kind of trap!"

Evie's hands went cold, and she took an involuntary step back, the implications of Miss Pearl's words settling heavily on her shoulders. She could hear the night sounds around them, crickets chirping, the rustling of the magnolia leaves in the breeze, but the world felt strangely distant, as if everything had been shifted slightly out of focus.

Grayson reached out, placing a hand on her arm, his grip warm and grounding. "Evie, it's okay," he said softly, though she could hear the concern in his voice. "We'll figure this out. Whatever's going on, you're not alone in it."

Evie nodded, but her gaze remained locked on Miss Pearl, who still looked as flustered as a hen caught in a rainstorm. "And you're absolutely sure, Miss Pearl? No tricks, no secret doors?"

Miss Pearl pressed a hand to her chest, her expression earnest and a little bit wounded. "I swear on my mother's best apple pie recipe, Evie. If I'd known you got stuck in that closet, I would've put a stop to all this right away. We may be meddlesome, but we're not heartless."

Evie let out a shaky breath, rubbing her temples as she tried to make sense of it all. "Okay... okay. I believe you, Miss Pearl. But that means there's something else going on in my shop that has nothing to do with you."

Grayson's expression hardened, and he straightened, his jaw set with determination. "Then we'll get to the bottom of it. I'll help you look into whatever this is, Evie. If there's something more than just old wiring and drafts in that building, we'll figure it out together."

Miss Pearl bit her lip, looking between them with a mixture of guilt and worry. "Oh, dear, I had no idea things had gotten this bad. I never meant for you to be frightened, Evie, truly. And I'll do whatever I can to make it right."

Evie managed a tired smile, even as her thoughts continued to race. "Thanks, Miss Pearl. Just... maybe ease up on the haunting tricks for a while, okay? I've got enough to deal with without any more surprises."

Miss Pearl nodded quickly, the relief evident on her face. "Of course, dear. No more rakes, I promise."

But as Evie and Grayson turned back toward the shop, the uneasy feeling lingered, creeping through the edges of her thoughts like a shadow that refused to fade. Whatever was happening at Iris & Ivy, it was clear that the matchmakers' meddling was only one piece of a much larger mystery.

And as they walked through the darkness, back toward the flower shop that seemed to hold more secrets than she'd ever imagined, Evie couldn't help but feel that the night's revelations were only the beginning.

Chapter 7

The morning sunlight streamed through the front windows of Iris & Ivy, casting a warm glow over the flower displays and the polished wood floors. Evie Matthews yawned as she flipped the "Closed" sign to "Open" and unlocked the door, trying to shake off the remnants of last night's strange events. The air still felt a little too cold, the shadows a little too deep, but she pushed the unease aside. She had a shop to run, and there were plenty of orders to fill.

She had just begun setting out a fresh arrangement of sunflowers when the doorbell jingled. Evie turned, expecting a customer, but instead, she found herself facing Miss Pearl, Betty, Ruby, and Hattie, each of them holding a tray or a basket piled high with baked goods.

Evie blinked in surprise as the women filed in, their arms laden with treats. Miss Pearl carried a plate of fudge brownies, Betty had a tray of blueberry muffins, Ruby balanced a large, triple chocolate cake in her arms, and Hattie held a plate of still-warm cinnamon rolls. They lined up in front of the counter, their expressions a mix of guilt and earnestness.

"Well, good morning, Evie, dear," Miss Pearl began, a sheepish smile tugging at her lips. "We thought we'd bring you a little something as a way of saying... well, you know... we're sorry."

Betty nodded eagerly, her red curls bouncing. "Yes, we are so, *so* sorry about all the trouble we caused, dear. We never meant to scare you so badly!"

Hattie, clutching her cinnamon rolls, looked genuinely distressed. "We were just trying to give you a little push toward Grayson, but we didn't realize it would go so far."

Ruby, who usually wore a smirk, looked surprisingly contrite as she set the chocolate cake down on the counter. "And, well, we thought maybe some sweets might make up for all the trouble. Triple chocolate, your favorite."

Evie took a step back, eyeing the mountain of baked goods with a mixture of bewilderment and amusement. She crossed her arms, raising an eyebrow as she regarded the quartet of guilty matchmakers. "So, this is your way of saying sorry, huh? Bribery with sugar?"

Miss Pearl gave a nervous little laugh, but her expression turned serious as she met Evie's gaze. "More like a peace offering, Evie. We really are sorry. We didn't realize how frightened you'd be, and we should have been more thoughtful."

The other women nodded, echoing their apologies in a chorus of remorseful murmurs. Evie looked at them for a long moment, her lips pursed, before finally letting out a slow breath. "Okay, I appreciate the apologies. But there's still something I need to know."

She leaned forward, her expression turning steely as she pinned each of them with a pointed look. "Did *any* of you have anything to do with locking Grayson and me in that closet? Did one of you set that up as part of your plan?"

The women glanced at each other, and for a moment, the only sound was the faint hum of the refrigerator in the back of the shop. Ruby looked genuinely bewildered, and Hattie's mouth fell open in shock.

"Good heavens, no!" Hattie gasped, clutching her chest as if she might faint. "Why, I'd never dream of doing something like that! Locking someone in a closet? Oh, I think I'm feeling faint just at the thought of it!"

Evie's eyes widened, and for a moment, she thought Hattie might actually swoon like some delicate Victorian lady. Betty reached out to steady her, patting Hattie's shoulder as she gave Evie a reproachful look.

"No, Evie, we wouldn't do that," Betty said, her tone earnest. "It's one thing to give you a little scare with some noises, but trapping you in a closet? That's not us. We had no idea that even happened."

Ruby shook her head, her expression as serious as Evie had ever seen it. "We might be nosy, but we're not reckless. Whatever happened with that closet, it wasn't part of our plan."

Evie studied their faces, searching for any hint of deceit, but all she saw was sincerity—and a fair amount of concern. Her shoulders sagged slightly, a sense of relief mingling with a fresh wave of confusion.

Miss Pearl spread her hands, her voice gentle but insistent. "Dear, we wouldn't lie to you about this, not after everything. And if there's something strange happening in that shop, well, we'd like to help you figure it out."

Evie sighed, running a hand through her messy ponytail as she tried to make sense of it all. "I don't know what to think anymore. One minute, I'm convinced it's all you meddling matchmakers, and the next, I'm hearing things I can't explain."

She glanced toward the back of the shop, where the shadows still seemed to linger longer than they should. For a moment, the air felt strangely still, and she thought she heard a faint, high-pitched giggle, like the sound of a child laughing from a distance.

Evie stiffened, turning sharply to face the matchmakers, but their expressions were blank, none of them seemed to have heard the sound. She shook her head, trying to dismiss it as her imagination, but a shiver ran down her spine all the same. "I really need to get out more." Evie muttered.

Miss Pearl took a step closer, her tone turning lighter, as if she sensed the need to change the subject. "Speaking of getting out, Evie dear, I was wondering, are you planning to attend the annual church's end of summer dance this weekend?"

Evie blinked, caught off guard by the abrupt change in topic. "The church dance? I haven't heard anything about it."

Ruby leaned forward, her expression earnest. "Oh, you must come! It's the biggest social event of the summer, dancing, live music, and the best potluck you'll ever see. It's the perfect way to get to know folks around here."

Betty nodded vigorously, her curls bobbing. "And it would be so good for your business, Evie. The whole town shows up, and everyone loves to see new faces. Why, I bet you'd have half the town ordering bouquets by Monday if they got to know you better."

Hattie, still clutching her chest, managed to offer a weak smile. "And who knows? You might just have a little fun, dear. You deserve a break after everything you've been through."

Evie hesitated, glancing at the eager faces surrounding her. "I don't know... I haven't been to a dance in years. And I don't exactly have a date, so..."

Miss Pearl waved her hand dismissively, her eyes twinkling with mischief again. "Oh, nonsense, child! You don't need a date to have a good time. Just come, enjoy yourself, and mingle a little. Who knows? Maybe you'll even run into a certain handsome neighbor while you're there."

Evie rolled her eyes, but a reluctant smile tugged at her lips. "Fine, fine, I'll think about it. But only if you promise not to try any more 'haunting' tricks in the meantime."

Miss Pearl raised a hand, her expression solemn. "You have my word, Evie. No more tricks. Just a few friendly faces trying to make amends."

Evie couldn't help but smile at the earnestness of their apologies, even if the whole situation still felt more than a little surreal. As the women gathered their empty trays and baskets, they offered her one last round of reassurances.

Evie watched the matchmakers leave, the bell above the door jingling softly as they stepped out into the morning sun, their arms laden with now-empty trays and baskets. She stood behind the counter, surrounded by a mountain of sweets, feeling a little like she'd just been caught up in a tornado of apologies and baked goods.

The smile lingered on her face, but as the door swung shut and the sounds of the town crept back in through the windows, her thoughts turned inward. She glanced around the flower shop, the shadows in the corners seeming a little darker than usual. The giggle she'd heard moments ago still echoed faintly in her mind, like the lingering notes of a distant melody. She shook her head, telling herself it had to be her imagination, the result of too little sleep and too many strange happenings. But deep down, she wasn't so sure.

Evie turned back to the counter, where the piles of brownies, muffins, and chocolate cake sat like a sugary peace offering. She couldn't help but let out a small, rueful laugh, imagining Miss Pearl and her friends plotting their apology over coffee and cinnamon rolls at Ruby's Diner. They might have caused her more trouble than she ever wanted, but their hearts were in the right place.

Still, the unease wouldn't leave her. She couldn't forget the look on Miss Pearl's face when she had asked about the closet, the genuine surprise, the wide-eyed disbelief. It had been as if the very idea of trapping someone inside was unthinkable to her.

Evie reached out and picked up a fudge brownie, taking a small bite as she tried to settle her thoughts. It was rich and sweet, the kind of chocolate that melted on her tongue, but even that comfort couldn't erase the nagging feeling that something else was going on. Something that had nothing to do with the matchmakers' schemes.

She glanced toward the back room, where the shadows seemed to stretch just a little longer than they should. For a brief moment, she considered calling Grayson again, just to have him come over and take another look around the shop. But she dismissed the thought just as quickly, reminding herself that she couldn't rely on him every time she got spooked by a noise.

No, she needed to handle this on her own, or at least figure out how to keep her wits about her until she understood what was happening.

She brushed the crumbs off her fingers and turned back to the day's work, determined to focus on the orders she needed to fill. As she arranged bouquets of roses and lilies, trying to lose herself in the familiar rhythm of trimming stems and arranging petals, the scent of sugar and chocolate filled the shop, mingling with the earthy fragrance of flowers.

But as the morning wore on, the feeling of being watched never quite left her. And more than once, she found herself glancing toward the shadows in the corners, half-expecting to see something, or someone, lurking just out of sight.

She pushed the thoughts away, trying to focus on the matchmakers' invitation instead. The church dance, with its promises of music and laughter, sounded like a nice break from the mysteries of Iris & Ivy. And maybe it would be good for business, just as Betty had said.

Of course, the idea of going alone still made her stomach twist with nerves. The last thing she wanted was to be the odd one out in a room full of happy couples, especially when she already felt like an outsider in Magnolia Springs. But then she thought of Grayson's easy smile, the way he'd looked at her that morning with quiet concern, and a part of her wondered if maybe he wouldn't mind going with her. As friends, of course.

But she brushed the thought away, focusing on tying a ribbon around a bouquet. She wasn't ready to open that door just yet, even if the idea made her heart beat a little faster.

The day passed in a blur of customers and deliveries, with Evie doing her best to keep her thoughts from wandering back to the mysteries of the shop. By the time evening rolled around, she was exhausted but a little more at ease, telling herself that maybe she'd imagined the worst of it. Maybe, just maybe, the strangeness would pass now that Miss Pearl and her friends had promised to back off.

But as she locked up the shop and headed upstairs to her apartment, the shadows seemed to shift behind her, and she could have sworn she heard that faint, airy giggle once more, a sound that sent chills racing down her spine, even as she told herself she was just hearing things.

Evie paused at the top of the stairs, looking back over her shoulder at the dim interior of Iris & Ivy. The moonlight filtered through the front windows, casting pale beams across the floor, and for a moment, she thought she saw a flicker of movement in the darkness. A whisper of motion, gone as quickly as it had come.

She shook her head, forcing herself to take a deep breath. "It's nothing, Evie," she whispered to herself, trying to make the words feel real. "Just your imagination. Just a draft, or the old building settling."

But even as she turned and closed the apartment door behind her, the unease lingered, curling around the edges of her thoughts like smoke.

Chapter 8

The morning sun was high in the sky when Clara swung open the door of Iris & Ivy, a mischievous smile already playing on her lips. The bell above the door jingled cheerfully, and Evie looked up from the bouquet she was arranging, a small but genuine smile spreading across her face.

"Hey, Clara," Evie said, dusting her hands off on her apron. "I didn't expect to see you so soon. What's up?"

Clara leaned casually against the counter, her hazel eyes twinkling. "Oh, nothing much, just checking in on my favorite flower shop owner. And, you know, I heard a little something about a certain dance happening this weekend."

Evie groaned softly, rolling her eyes. "Please don't tell me you're going to start in on me like Miss Pearl and her friends. I already got the 'you have to go' speech this morning, complete with about ten pounds of baked goods."

Clara laughed, the sound warm and familiar. "Well, I wouldn't be much of a friend if I didn't at least ask if you're planning on going. It's the biggest social event of the season, you know."

Evie sighed, leaning her hip against the counter as she wiped a smudge of dirt from her cheek. "I don't know, Clara. It's just... it's not really my scene, you know? Besides, I don't have a date, and it'd be awkward showing up alone."

Clara's smile turned sly, and she tilted her head, fixing Evie with a knowing look. "You know, you could always ask Grayson."

Evie's eyes widened, and she shook her head vehemently. "Oh no, I couldn't do that! I mean, he's already done so much for me, coming over to check out all the weird noises, getting locked in a closet with me, he probably thinks I'm a complete mess. I wouldn't want to bother him with something like this."

Clara raised an eyebrow, crossing her arms as she studied Evie. "Are you sure about that? Because from where I'm standing, it seems like he doesn't mind helping you out. In fact, I think he kind of likes being around you."

Evie's cheeks flushed, and she busied herself with rearranging a few roses in the bouquet. "You're imagining things, Clara. He's just being nice because we're neighbors, that's all. Besides, even if he did want to go to the dance, he probably already has a date lined up."

Clara made a dismissive sound, waving her hand. "Please. Magnolia Springs isn't exactly a hotbed of eligible bachelors and bachelorettes. I think you might be underestimating your own charm, Evie."

Evie shot her a skeptical look, but Clara just smiled brightly, refusing to be discouraged. "Look, all I'm saying is that you should think about it. You never know, he might surprise you. And if you decide you're brave enough to ask him, well, it could be fun."

Evie let out a reluctant laugh, though she still looked doubtful. "I'll think about it. But don't get your hopes up, okay?"

Clara grinned, patting her on the shoulder. "That's all I ask, my friend. And don't worry, I'll check back in with you later to make sure you're still in one piece after all those haunting scares."

Evie rolled her eyes again, but there was warmth behind her exasperation. "Yeah, yeah, I'll be fine. Thanks, Clara."

With a final wave, Clara headed out of the flower shop, but as soon as she stepped outside, her smile took on a more determined edge. She had another stop to make before her day was done, and if she played her cards right, she might just give fate a little nudge in the right direction.

The bell over the door at Grayson's hardware store chimed as Clara stepped inside. The store smelled faintly of sawdust and oil, and the aisles were lined with tools, paint cans, and every kind of hardware imaginable. Grayson stood behind the counter, unpacking a box of supplies, but he looked up with a smile when he saw Clara walk in.

"Well, if it isn't Magnolia Springs' busiest social butterfly," he said, setting down the box. "What brings you by, Clara?"

Clara leaned casually against the counter, folding her arms with a smile that was equal parts friendly and cunning. "Oh, just thought I'd see how you're doing, Grayson. And, you know, there's this dance coming up, in case you hadn't heard."

Grayson's brows lifted slightly, and he chuckled. "Yeah, I heard about it. Half the town's been talking about it all week. I'll probably stop by for a bit, can't hurt to make an appearance, right?"

Clara's smile widened, and she tilted her head, giving him a pointed look. "You know, it might be nice if you had a date to the dance."

Grayson blinked, clearly caught off guard by the suggestion. "A date?"

"Yeah," Clara said lightly, as if the idea had only just occurred to her. "You know, Evie's new in town, and she's been through a lot lately with the whole haunting thing. It might be nice if you asked her to go with you. She could probably use a friendly face by her side."

Grayson's ears turned a little pink, and he rubbed the back of his neck awkwardly. "I don't know, Clara. I mean, Evie's been through a lot. She might not want me tagging along and making things more complicated."

Clara raised an eyebrow, giving him a look that said she wasn't buying it for a second. "Oh, come on, Grayson. You get along great with Evie, and I think she'd be thrilled if you asked her. What's the worst that could happen?"

Grayson shifted his weight, clearly torn between the desire to ask Evie out and his own uncertainty. "I just don't want her to feel like I'm...

I don't know, pushing things too fast. We've barely known each other a few weeks."

Clara waved a dismissive hand. "Trust me, Grayson, she could use the company, and I think she'd appreciate the gesture. Besides, it's just a dance, no one's talking about wedding bells."

Grayson chuckled softly, though the pink in his cheeks deepened. "Well, when you put it that way... maybe you're right. I guess I could ask her."

Clara beamed, giving him an encouraging pat on the arm. "That's the spirit! Just be yourself, Grayson. You're a good guy, and Evie knows that."

Grayson nodded, a small, nervous smile tugging at his lips. "Yeah. I'll think about it. Thanks, Clara."

Clara winked at him, already turning toward the door with a spring in her step. "Anytime, Grayson. You know where to find me if you need more matchmaking advice!"

She left the hardware store with a satisfied smile, her plan humming along nicely in the back of her mind. As she walked down the sun-dappled streets of Magnolia Springs, she couldn't help but feel a thrill of excitement at the thought of her two friends sharing a night at the dance.

Maybe she was meddling, just a little. But as far as Clara was concerned, sometimes people needed a little push to find their way to each other, and she was more than happy to provide that nudge.

The lunch rush at Ruby's Diner was in full swing when Evie stepped inside, the familiar hum of conversation and the clinking of plates filling the air. This time, though, there was no sudden silence, no awkward stares from the matchmakers huddled in their usual booth. Instead, everyone seemed caught up in their own conversations, laughter bubbling through the cozy space. It was as if, for once, she wasn't the main topic of discussion.

Evie let out a breath she hadn't realized she was holding, feeling a little more at ease as she scanned the diner. She slid into an empty booth near the window, settling her purse on the seat beside her. It felt good to blend into the background for a change, to feel like just another face in the crowd. She picked up the menu, even though she knew it by heart, and pretended to study the specials written on the chalkboard.

But just as she was starting to relax, the bell above the door jingled, and she glanced up reflexively. Her breath caught when she saw Grayson walk in, his broad shoulders filling the doorway. He paused for a moment, scanning the room, and when his gaze landed on her, a smile curved his lips.

Evie's cheeks warmed unexpectedly, and she quickly looked back down at her menu, hoping to compose herself before he reached her table. She heard the soft scuff of his boots on the tiled floor as he approached, and then his shadow fell across the table.

"Hi, Evie," Grayson said, his voice warm and friendly. "You doing okay? Any more hauntings? Anything I need to check out?"

Evie glanced up at him, managing a small, sheepish smile. "No, no more strange noises... for now, anyway. I think Miss Pearl and her friends have decided to give me a break."

Grayson chuckled, his smile widening as he slid into the booth across from her. "Well, that's good to hear. Mind if I join you for lunch?"

Evie hesitated for a heartbeat, still feeling a little self-conscious about the way her heart seemed to pick up speed whenever he was around. But she quickly brushed the thought aside, gesturing to the empty seat. "Sure, go ahead."

Grayson settled in, resting his elbows on the table as he glanced out the window, his expression relaxed. "Beautiful day out there, isn't it? Almost makes you forget it's almost October."

Evie nodded, grateful for the casual conversation. "Yeah, the weather's been perfect. I've been thinking of setting up a little outdoor display at the shop, maybe some fall wreaths to draw in more of the foot traffic."

They chatted easily, the conversation flowing between them with a comfortable familiarity. Grayson asked her about her plans for Iris & Ivy, and Evie found herself talking about her hopes for the shop in a way she hadn't shared with anyone before. It was nice, she realized, to have someone who seemed genuinely interested in her life, even the small details.

Their waitress appeared, taking their orders, Grayson opted for a hearty cheeseburger with a side of fries, while Evie stuck with her favorite chicken salad sandwich. As the waitress walked away, Grayson leaned back in his seat, watching Evie with a thoughtful look in his eyes.

"So," he began casually, as if he'd only just thought of the question, "are you planning to go to the church dance this weekend?"

Evie blinked, caught off guard by the sudden shift in conversation. She felt her cheeks heat up again, and she fiddled with the edge of her napkin. "Oh, um, I'm not sure. I mean, I hadn't really planned on it. It's been a while since I went to anything like that."

Grayson nodded slowly, but there was a hint of a smile playing at the corners of his mouth. "Well, if you do decide to go... I was wondering if you'd like to go with me?"

Evie's mouth fell open slightly, and she stared at him for a moment, feeling completely blindsided. Her face turned an even brighter shade of pink, and she quickly ducked her head, trying to gather her thoughts. "I... you want to go to the dance with *me*?"

Grayson chuckled softly, rubbing the back of his neck, and for a moment, he looked almost shy. "Yeah, I thought it might be nice. I mean, if you'd like to. No pressure or anything."

Evie's mind raced, but before she could overthink it, she found herself nodding. "Okay. Yeah, I'd like that."

Grayson's smile grew, and he relaxed visibly, leaning forward a little. "Great. I'll pick you up at seven o'clock on Saturday night, then."

Evie's heart fluttered in a way she hadn't felt in a long time, and she couldn't help but smile back at him. "Seven o'clock sounds perfect."

The conversation moved on to lighter topics after that, Grayson told her about a new shipment coming into the hardware store, and Evie filled him in on the latest gossip she'd overheard from Miss Pearl and her friends. They laughed and shared stories, and by the time their food arrived, the initial awkwardness had melted away, replaced by an easy camaraderie that felt almost like... well, almost like the beginnings of something more.

They finished their lunch, Grayson's insistence on paying for both, and then they stepped outside into the sunny afternoon. The air was warm, and for a moment, they lingered on the sidewalk in front of the diner, neither of them quite ready to say goodbye.

"I'll see you Saturday, then?" Grayson asked, giving her a lopsided smile that made her heart skip a beat.

Evie nodded, feeling a little breathless despite herself. "Yeah, I'll see you then. Thanks for lunch, Grayson. It was... it was nice."

Grayson's expression softened, and he reached out, giving her shoulder a gentle squeeze. "Anytime, Evie. Take care, okay?"

With that, he turned and walked back toward his hardware store, his tall figure casting a long shadow in the afternoon sun. Evie watched him go, a smile tugging at her lips despite the flutter of nerves in her chest. She turned back toward Iris & Ivy, trying to ignore the way her heart seemed to be dancing in her chest.

But as she glanced back through the diner window, her smile faded as she caught sight of something that made her do a double-take. Clara was standing near the back of the diner, and she had just sidled up to Miss Pearl, a smug grin on her face. Without any attempt to hide it, Clara raised her hand, and Miss Pearl met it with a triumphant high-five.

Evie blinked, her mind racing as she tried to process what she had just seen. Clara's expression was one of pure satisfaction, and Miss Pearl's smile was as wide as Evie had ever seen it. They looked like two kids who had just pulled off the ultimate prank.

"What on earth was that about?" Evie muttered under her breath, narrowing her eyes as she watched Clara and Miss Pearl chat animatedly.

A small suspicion nagged at the back of her mind, but she quickly shook her head, deciding she'd deal with it later. After all, she had a dance to look forward to, and for the first time in weeks, she felt like maybe, just maybe, things were starting to look up.

With a final glance over her shoulder, she headed back toward her shop, wondering what exactly her friend and Miss Pearl were up to, and whether she'd ever truly understand the strange, meddling ways of Magnolia Springs.

Chapter 9

The sun was beginning to set over Magnolia Springs, casting long shadows across the town square as Miss Pearl gathered her trusted companions, Betty, Ruby, and Hattie, in her cozy living room. They settled into their favorite seats, each clutching a cup of tea, and the air buzzed with anticipation. Tonight, they were convening for a very specific purpose: to advance their latest matchmaking scheme for Evie and Grayson.

Miss Pearl set her teacup down on the coffee table with a decisive clink, smoothing her floral skirt as she looked around at her friends. "Ladies, we've done a good job so far. Evie's agreed to go to the dance with Grayson, and she seems to be warming up to the idea of him being more than just a helpful neighbor."

Betty nodded eagerly, her curls bouncing with enthusiasm. "And did you see the way she looked at him when he walked into the diner earlier? Like she didn't quite know what to do with herself. They're as sweet as pie together!"

Hattie, always the most cautious of the group, adjusted her glasses and glanced at Miss Pearl. "That's all well and good, Pearl, but we can't leave things to chance. What if they get to the dance and just end up standing around like two shy teenagers at their first prom? We need to give them a little... nudge."

Ruby, leaning back in her armchair with a smirk, raised an eyebrow. "What did you have in mind, Hattie? I mean, we've already tried the haunted shop trick, and that didn't go quite as planned."

Miss Pearl chuckled, waving a dismissive hand. "Oh, that's behind us now, Ruby. And besides, I've got a new idea that's a little more... subtle. Well, subtle for us, anyway."

She reached into the knitting basket beside her chair and pulled out a small, folded paper, handing it to Betty. Betty unfolded it carefully, her eyes widening as she read the contents. "Pearl, are you sure about this? I mean, it's a little bit sneaky, even for us."

Miss Pearl gave a knowing smile, her eyes twinkling with mischief. "It's not sneaky, Betty, it's strategic. Evie and Grayson have already taken the first step by agreeing to go to the dance together, but we need to make sure they actually *enjoy* themselves, and each other, once they're there."

Hattie leaned forward, peering over Betty's shoulder at the paper. "What is it? What's the plan?"

Betty turned the paper around, revealing a list written in Miss Pearl's neat, looping handwriting. At the top, in bold letters, were the words *Dance Competition Pairings*.

Ruby's smirk widened into a full grin, and she let out a low chuckle. "Now this is more like it. A little friendly competition always gets people talking, and dancing. But how are we going to make sure they're paired together?"

Miss Pearl settled back in her chair, looking thoroughly pleased with herself. "That's where I come in. You see, I had a little chat with Pastor Stevens earlier today, and I volunteered to help with the organizing. And wouldn't you know it? He thought it was a fine idea to have a dance competition to liven things up. I just so happened to suggest that we draw names to pair people up."

Hattie's eyes widened, and she clapped her hands together in delight. "Oh, Pearl, you sly thing! So you're going to rig the drawing so Evie and Grayson end up as partners?"

Miss Pearl pressed a finger to her lips, though her smile gave away her satisfaction. "Let's just say I'll have a hand in ensuring that particular pairing. And once they're out there on the dance floor, twirling and laughing, they won't be able to resist the sparks that are bound to fly."

Betty leaned in, her excitement growing. "But won't they catch on that we're behind it? Evie's no fool, and she's already a little suspicious of us after the whole haunting incident."

Miss Pearl's smile softened, turning more thoughtful. "Maybe she will, eventually. But by the time she does, it won't matter, because she'll already be having the time of her life with Grayson. And they'll both see that there's something real between them, something worth exploring."

Ruby raised her teacup in a toast, a mischievous gleam in her eye. "Here's to Operation Dance Partners, then. Let's make sure Evie and Grayson have the best, and most unexpected, night of their lives."

The women clinked their cups together, sealing their next move with the enthusiasm of a group of teenagers plotting their first adventure. They knew they were meddling, and they knew that things might not go perfectly according to plan. But they also knew that sometimes, love needed a little push in the right direction. And if that push involved a bit of creative maneuvering behind the scenes, well, then they were more than happy to oblige.

Miss Pearl leaned back in her chair, taking a slow, satisfied sip of her tea as the laughter and planning swirled around her. It was moments like this, when she could feel the energy of her friends coming together for a common goal that made her love being a part of Magnolia Springs.

"Now, listen up," Miss Pearl said, regaining their attention as she pulled out another folded sheet of paper from her knitting basket. "This here is the list of everyone who's already signed up for the dance competition. We need to make sure that Evie's and Grayson's names just so happen to be drawn together."

Ruby took the list, skimming through it with a wry smile. "Good thing most of the town doesn't mind a little fun and games. I'll bet folks will love the idea of a dance contest, and even more if it means a few surprises along the way."

Hattie adjusted her glasses, a worried frown crossing her face. "But what if Evie says no to the competition? You know how she can be, she might not want to make a big scene."

Miss Pearl's eyes twinkled. "Leave that to me, Hattie. I'll make sure she gets caught up in the excitement. Besides, once she sees that Grayson's her partner, I think she'll be too flustered to back out."

Betty giggled, clapping her hands together with delight. "Oh, I can just picture it now! Evie trying to keep her composure while Grayson twirls her around the dance floor. And you know how good he is with that country two-step, she won't stand a chance."

Ruby's smirk widened as she leaned back in her chair. "I think our real challenge will be keeping ourselves from laughing too loud when it all goes down."

Miss Pearl couldn't help but chuckle at the image of the dance contest playing out. But beneath the humor, there was a genuine warmth in her smile. She thought of Evie, new to Magnolia Springs and struggling to find her place, and Grayson, who'd been a steady presence in town but had kept mostly to himself in recent years.

"Evie deserves a little joy, after all she's been through," Miss Pearl said, her tone turning thoughtful. "And Grayson, well, he's been too serious for too long. Maybe this dance is just what they both need to shake things up a little."

Betty's expression softened, and she nodded in agreement. "You're right, Pearl. Sometimes people just need a chance to see what's been right in front of them all along."

Hattie adjusted her glasses, a determined look in her eyes. "And we're just the folks to make sure they get that chance."

They spent the next half hour fine-tuning their plan, with Miss Pearl giving detailed instructions on how the drawing would be set up. Ruby volunteered to take charge of the paper slips, ensuring that Evie and Grayson's names would be the ones pulled from the hat. Betty promised to bake a special batch of cookies for the event, to make sure everyone stayed sweet and distracted. And Hattie, always the planner, took careful notes to make sure no detail was overlooked.

As the evening wore on, the living room filled with laughter and the warmth of their shared excitement. Outside, the stars began to twinkle over the quiet streets of Magnolia Springs, casting a soft glow over the town that the matchmakers knew so well.

When the planning finally wrapped up, Miss Pearl walked her friends to the door, each of them stepping out onto the porch with their baskets and bags. They exchanged goodbyes, their smiles lingering in the cool night air, before heading off in different directions.

Miss Pearl stood on her porch for a moment longer, watching as her friends disappeared down the sleepy streets, their laughter fading into the distance. She glanced back toward the lights of the town square, her thoughts drifting to the dance that lay just a few days away.

"I hope you're ready, Evie," she murmured to herself, a satisfied smile playing at the corners of her mouth. "Because you're about to get swept off your feet, one way or another."

With that, she turned and headed back inside, closing the door behind her with a soft click. The house settled around her, warm and familiar, but she couldn't quite shake the thrill of anticipation that hummed in her chest.

Miss Pearl knew better than anyone that life in Magnolia Springs had a way of surprising you when you least expected it. And if she had anything to do with it, Evie Matthews and Grayson Bennett were in for a surprise they wouldn't soon forget.

Chapter 10

The sun dipped low on the horizon, casting a warm, golden glow over Magnolia Springs as Grayson Bennett drove his old pickup down the quiet streets. The air held a slight chill, but Grayson barely noticed the cold. His mind was on the woman he was about to pick up, and the dance that had turned into far more than just a small-town event.

He pulled up in front of Iris & Ivy, the flower shop's windows glowing softly in the twilight. His hands gripped the steering wheel for a moment before he took a deep breath, smoothing down the front of his freshly pressed shirt. He'd opted for a deep blue button-up that his sister had insisted brought out the color of his eyes, paired with his nicest pair of jeans and a leather jacket that he rarely wore. He glanced in the side mirror, brushing a hand through his dark hair in an attempt to tame the unruly curls, and then climbed out of the truck.

The old gravel crunched under his boots as he walked up to the shop's door. He paused, glancing up at the windows of the apartment above the flower shop, where a faint shadow moved behind the curtains. He could feel the nerves stirring in his gut, something he hadn't felt in years, and he knocked lightly on the door.

A moment later, the door swung open, and Evie stepped out, looking like a vision in a flowing blue dress that seemed to catch the last rays of the setting sun. Her auburn hair was loosely curled, falling over her shoulders in soft waves, and she wore just a touch of makeup that brought out the green of her eyes. She looked elegant and effortless, a contrast to her usual casual style, and for a moment, Grayson could only stare.

"You look... amazing, Evie," he managed, finding his voice at last.

Evie's cheeks flushed a light pink, and she brushed a hand over the skirt of her dress, as if smoothing out an invisible wrinkle. "Thanks, Grayson. You look pretty nice yourself."

He smiled, feeling some of the tension ease from his shoulders. He offered his arm to her, and after a moment's hesitation, she took it, her hand warm against his sleeve. They walked together to his truck, the night air cool against their faces, and he opened the passenger door for her with a small flourish that earned him a laugh.

The drive to the church hall wasn't long, but Grayson took his time, wanting to savor the quiet moments before they stepped into the swirl of the evening. As they passed through the town square, he pointed out a few landmarks, filling the silence with easy conversation.

"See that little shop over there?" Grayson nodded toward a quaint brick building with a green awning. "That's Martha's bookstore. She used to be the town librarian before she retired, but she couldn't quite give up her love for books. If you ever need a recommendation, she's your woman. Knows every author from here to New York."

Evie leaned forward slightly, peering out the window at the bookstore's cozy display of hardcovers and paperbacks. "I'll have to check it out sometime. I didn't even realize we had a bookstore in town."

Grayson chuckled, glancing at her with a teasing smile. "That's Magnolia Springs for you, full of surprises. Like that café you like so much? Ruby's been running that place since her husband passed, oh, about ten years ago. She's the one who keeps the town caffeinated and keeps Miss Pearl from meddling too much. Well, most of the time, anyway."

Evie laughed softly, and for a moment, the conversation flowed easily between them as they talked about the town, its quirks, and the people they were beginning to share their lives with. By the time they reached the church hall, she was feeling more at ease, the tension of the past few days slipping away like the last traces of daylight.

Grayson pulled up beside a line of cars and helped her down from the truck, guiding her toward the entrance with a hand on her elbow. The hall was aglow with strings of fairy lights, casting a warm, inviting light over the gathering crowd. Music drifted out through the open doors, a cheerful country tune that had toes tapping and heads bobbing.

As they stepped inside, Evie took in the scene with wide eyes. The space had been transformed with decorations, autumn garlands draped over the walls, hay bales lining the dance floor, and pumpkins carved with intricate designs glowing from every corner. The band played on a small stage at the far end, their music filling the air with a lively beat that made it impossible not to smile.

Grayson leaned closer, speaking over the music. "You doing okay?"

Evie nodded, her nerves fading into the background. "Yeah. It's... really nice, actually. I didn't know the town could come together like this."

Grayson's smile softened. "It's one of the things I love about this place. Everyone shows up, no matter what."

He led her further into the hall, where clusters of townsfolk gathered around tables laden with potluck dishes. Evie spotted a few familiar faces, but there were many she hadn't met before. As they wove through the crowd, Grayson made introductions, pointing out each new person with the ease of someone who'd grown up in the town.

"That there's Kevin Ridley," he said, nodding toward a tall, wiry man with a shock of sandy hair and a lopsided grin. Kevin wore a well-worn flannel shirt and jeans, and he seemed to be in the middle of telling a joke that had a group of farmers roaring with laughter. "He runs the biggest corn farm on this side of the county. Likes to tell folks he's got the best corn whiskey too, but don't ask him about it unless you're prepared to listen for an hour."

Kevin caught sight of them and raised a hand in greeting, his grin widening. "Hey there, Grayson! Nice to see you brought some class to this shindig tonight."

Evie smiled back, charmed by Kevin's easy manner. "Nice to meet you, Kevin. I'll have to talk you into telling me about your corn whiskey sometime."

Kevin winked. "Anytime, Miss Evie. And Grayson, you better take good care of her tonight, you hear?"

Grayson rolled his eyes good-naturedly, steering Evie away before Kevin could launch into another story. They passed a petite woman with curly gray hair who was fussing over a table of cookies, and Grayson nodded toward her with a fond smile. "That's Helen Lawson, she owns the bakery on Maple Street. Oh, and she makes the best pecan pie in town."

Helen looked up, her face lighting up when she saw them. "Oh, you two make such a lovely pair! Make sure you try some of the snickerdoodles, dear, they're fresh out of the oven."

Evie blushed, feeling a little self-conscious under Helen's knowing gaze, but she couldn't help but smile. "Thank you, Helen. I will."

They continued through the crowd, meeting everyone from Gary, the town barber who always had a story about Magnolia Springs' colorful history, to Tina, a bubbly kindergarten teacher who insisted on hugging everyone she met. Each new face seemed to come with its own story, and Evie found herself falling a little more in love with the town with every introduction.

After a while, Grayson led her toward the dance floor, glancing down at her with a hopeful smile. "Think you're up for a dance?"

Evie hesitated, glancing around the bustling room, but then she caught the encouraging smiles of the townsfolk watching them, and she nodded. "Okay. Let's give it a try."

Grayson's grin widened, and he took her hand, leading her onto the dance floor as the band struck up a slow, swaying tune. He wrapped an arm around her waist, holding her close but not too close, and they began to move in time with the music. At first, Evie felt stiff and self-conscious, aware of every step and stumble, but Grayson's steady presence kept her grounded.

They moved through a few songs, chatting between twirls and steps. Grayson told her about his childhood, how he used to sneak into the barn dances when he was too young to join in, and Evie shared stories of her aunt Iris, who used to throw impromptu garden parties in the backyard. It was easy and light, but underneath it, Evie could feel something deeper, an understanding that she hadn't expected to find.

But just as she was starting to enjoy herself, the music faded, and Miss Pearl's voice rang through the hall, amplified by the microphone she held. "Ladies and gentlemen, if I could have your attention, please!"

Evie glanced toward the stage, where Miss Pearl stood, flanked by Betty, Ruby, and Hattie, each of them wearing expressions that bordered on gleeful. Evie couldn't shake the feeling that something was about to happen, something orchestrated by the matchmakers.

"It's time for the annual dance competition!" Miss Pearl declared, her voice carrying easily over the crowd. "And this year, we're doing things a little differently. We'll be pairing up our dancers by drawing names out of a hat!"

The crowd buzzed with excitement, and Grayson turned to Evie with a wry smile. "Think we'll get lucky?"

Evie chuckled, feeling the nerves return. "With Miss Pearl in charge, who knows?"

Miss Pearl reached into a large hat, her expression the picture of innocence as she drew out a slip of paper. "Our first pair is... Evie Matthews

Miss Pearl reached into a large hat, her expression the picture of innocence as she drew out another slip of paper. "Our first pair is... Evie Matthews and Grayson Bennett!"

Evie's heart skipped a beat, and she turned to Grayson, her eyes wide with surprise. He looked equally taken aback, but a slow smile spread across his face. "Looks like we're partners again."

Evie forced a laugh, feeling a flutter of nerves in her chest. "Yeah, I guess we are."

Miss Pearl continued to call out pairs, but Evie couldn't focus on the names. Her mind was spinning with the unexpected turn of events, and she couldn't shake the feeling that this was all part of Miss Pearl's grand plan. As she glanced back at the stage, she caught sight of Ruby giving her a thumbs-up and Hattie shooting her a wink.

The band struck up a lively tune, and Grayson held out his hand, a playful grin on his face. "Shall we?"

Evie hesitated for a moment, but then she took his hand, letting him lead her back onto the dance floor. The music picked up, a fast-paced two-step that had couples spinning and twirling around them, and Grayson pulled her close, guiding her into the rhythm of the dance.

At first, Evie felt like her feet were moving too fast, her steps stumbling over the quick beat, but Grayson's hand was steady at her back, and his laughter was warm in her ear. "Relax, Evie. Just follow my lead."

She took a deep breath, focusing on the feel of his hand in hers, the way his grip was firm but gentle, and the easy confidence in his steps. Slowly, she found herself falling into the rhythm, matching his movements as he spun her around the floor.

They twirled through the room, weaving between the other couples, and Evie felt a laugh bubble up in her chest. The music seemed to lift her off her feet, carrying her through the steps, and she couldn't help but smile up at Grayson, who was watching her with a look of pure enjoyment.

"There you go," he said, his voice just loud enough to hear over the music. "You're a natural."

Evie shook her head, but she couldn't stop smiling. "I don't know about that, but... it's a lot more fun than I expected."

Grayson grinned, and for a moment, the world seemed to narrow down to just the two of them, the music and the movement, the warmth of his hand in hers. The rest of the hall faded into the background, and Evie found herself wishing that the song would last just a little bit longer.

But all too soon, the music slowed, and the dance came to an end. They were both slightly breathless as they stepped off the dance floor, the applause and cheers of the crowd ringing in their ears. Grayson kept his arm around her as they made their way back to their seats, and Evie was acutely aware of the way his hand lingered at her waist, the casual familiarity of the gesture.

She caught sight of Miss Pearl watching them from across the room, her expression smugly satisfied, and Evie couldn't help but shoot her a narrowed look. Miss Pearl simply winked back, clearly unrepentant.

As they took their seats, the band shifted to a slower tune, and the rest of the couples took to the dance floor. Grayson leaned back in his chair, glancing over at Evie with a thoughtful look in his eyes. "So... what do you think? Did you have a good time?"

Evie considered the question, and despite the nerves and the unexpected pairing, she realized that she had. The night had been full of surprises, but in a way, it had also been exactly what she needed, a chance to let go, to laugh, and to feel like a part of the town she was starting to call home.

She smiled at him, her expression softening. "Yeah, Grayson, I really did. Thanks for being my dance partner. And for... everything, really."

Grayson's smile widened, and for a moment, he looked almost boyish, his usual reserved manner giving way to something warmer. "You're welcome, Evie. I'm glad I got to share it with you."

They stayed for a few more songs, chatting and enjoying the easy atmosphere of the hall, but eventually, Grayson noticed that Evie was beginning to look a little tired, and he offered to take her home. She agreed, and they made their way back to the truck, saying goodbye to the townsfolk who lingered by the punch bowl and the dessert table.

The drive back to Iris & Ivy was quiet, the truck's headlights casting long beams over the empty streets. Grayson pulled up in front of the flower shop, turning off the engine and stepping out to walk her to the door. The night air had grown colder, and Evie wrapped her arms around herself as they walked up the steps.

When they reached the door, she turned to face him, feeling a little awkward but grateful all the same. "Thank you, Grayson. For everything tonight. It... really meant a lot."

Grayson smiled, his expression softening as he met her gaze. "It was my pleasure, Evie. I don't think I've had that much fun at a dance in years."

For a moment, they stood there in the soft glow of the porch light, the silence stretching between them in a way that felt both comfortable and charged with something unspoken. Then, before she could overthink it, Grayson leaned down and pressed a gentle kiss to her cheek, his lips warm against her skin.

Evie's breath caught, her cheeks heating up at the unexpected gesture. When he pulled back, there was a hint of color in his own cheeks, and he rubbed the back of his neck, looking a little sheepish.

"Goodnight, Evie," he said, his voice low and sincere. "I'll see you soon."

Evie nodded, her hand hovering near the door handle, but she couldn't help but smile at him, feeling a warmth spread through her chest that had nothing to do with the cool night air. "Goodnight, Grayson."

As he walked back to his truck, Evie watched him go, feeling a flutter in her chest that she hadn't felt in a long time. She touched her cheek where his kiss had landed, a small, shy smile tugging at her lips as she stepped inside the shop.

But just as she closed the door behind her, she thought she heard the faint sound of a giggle, so soft that it could have been the wind. She froze, glancing around the darkened shop, but there was nothing out of place, just the flowers quietly resting in their vases and the shadows pooling in the corners.

Evie shook her head, telling herself it was just her imagination, but she couldn't quite shake the feeling that there was something, or someone, still watching over her. And as she made her way upstairs to her apartment, the warmth of Grayson's kiss lingered on her cheek, mingling with the sense of mystery that seemed to follow her like a shadow.

Chapter 11

The morning sun had barely crested the horizon when Magnolia Springs came alive with whispers and rumors. The cool air was filled with the scent of freshly baked goods from Helen's bakery, mingling with the familiar earthy aroma of the town square after a night of autumn rain. But there was something new in the air that morning, something that had every shopkeeper, farmer, and local busybody buzzing with excitement: the gossip about the previous night's dance.

Specifically, the kiss between Evie Matthews and Grayson Bennett.

Evie, completely unaware of the town's new favorite topic, made her way down the stairs of Iris & Ivy, the flower shop still quiet in the early hours. She yawned as she unlocked the front door and flipped the sign to "Open." As she arranged a fresh bouquet of chrysanthemums in the display window, she tried to focus on her work, but her thoughts kept drifting back to the dance, to the warmth of Grayson's hand in hers, and that sweet, unexpected kiss on her cheek as he'd said goodnight.

She pressed a hand to her cheek, feeling the heat rise to her face again just thinking about it. "Get it together, Evie," she muttered to herself, shaking her head. "It was just a friendly gesture, nothing more."

But even as she tried to convince herself, a part of her couldn't help but wonder if maybe, just maybe, there had been more to it.

The bell above the door jingled, pulling her from her thoughts, and she turned to see Clara, her friend, striding into the shop with a knowing grin. Clara's dark hair was pulled back into a messy bun, and she wore her usual jeans and a cozy sweater, but her expression was anything but casual.

"Well, well, well, look who's up bright and early," Clara teased, leaning casually against the counter. "How are you feeling this morning, Evie? Get any sleep last night, or were you too busy thinking about a certain tall, handsome neighbor?"

Evie's cheeks flushed even redder, and she turned back to the bouquet, trying to hide her embarrassment. "I don't know what you're talking about, Clara. It was just a kiss on the cheek, no big deal."

Clara raised an eyebrow, folding her arms with a smirk. "Oh, sure. No big deal. That's why the whole town's been talking about it since sunrise."

Evie froze, her hands going still among the flowers. "Wait, what do you mean the whole town's talking about it?"

Clara's grin widened, and she leaned in closer, dropping her voice to a conspiratorial whisper. "Oh, you have *no* idea. I stopped by Ruby's for coffee this morning, and you should've heard them. Miss Pearl, Betty, and the rest of the gang were practically giddy. And they weren't the only ones, and Helen's already baking a 'Kiss of the Century' pie to commemorate the occasion."

Evie groaned, burying her face in her hands. "You've got to be kidding me. It was just a *kiss on the cheek*. How did this turn into a town-wide event?"

Clara patted her on the back, barely hiding her amusement. "Welcome to Magnolia Springs, Evie. Where even the smallest spark turns into a wildfire of gossip. You should've known better than to kiss Grayson Bennett in front of half the town."

Evie peeked out from between her fingers, her expression a mix of horror and resignation. "I didn't even kiss him! He kissed *me!*"

Clara shrugged, her smile never wavering. "Details, details. Trust me, they don't care about that part. They're just thrilled to have something new to talk about. And honestly, can you blame them? It's not every day that one of the town's most eligible bachelor's shows interest in our lovely new florist."

Evie sighed, letting her hands fall to her sides. "This is a nightmare. What am I supposed to do, Clara? I can't go anywhere without everyone looking at me like I'm some kind of romantic heroine."

Clara's expression softened, and she gave Evie a reassuring nudge. "Just ride it out, Evie. These things blow over eventually. And hey, it's not all bad, at least now everyone knows you're not just that new girl hiding behind the flowers. You're practically a local celebrity."

Evie groaned again, but despite her embarrassment, she couldn't help but laugh at the absurdity of it all. "Yeah, a celebrity for getting kissed. Great."

Meanwhile, across town at Ruby's Diner, the morning rush was in full swing, and the gossip was flowing as freely as the coffee. Miss Pearl and her friends occupied their usual booth, their voices carrying through the room as they recounted every detail of the dance.

"I told you it would work," Miss Pearl declared triumphantly, taking a sip of her coffee. "You should have seen the way Grayson looked at her when they were dancing. I haven't seen him smile like that in ages."

Betty leaned in, her eyes sparkling. "And did you see how flustered Evie was when he kissed her goodnight? I swear, I thought she was going to faint right there on the spot."

Hattie fanned herself with a napkin, nodding vigorously. "Oh, it was just like one of those romance novels you get at the library, Pearl. You know, the kind where the heroine doesn't realize she's falling in love until it's too late."

Ruby, carrying a fresh pot of coffee, rolled her eyes but couldn't hide her own smile. "Now don't you go scaring them off, ladies. We want them to have a chance, don't we?"

Miss Pearl raised a hand, her expression mock-serious. "Of course, Ruby. We wouldn't dream of meddling any more than we already have."

The other women laughed, and even Ruby couldn't help but chuckle. But beneath the humor, there was a sense of genuine warmth in their voices, a shared hope that maybe, just maybe, they had helped bring a little bit of happiness to two people who deserved it.

And as they chatted and sipped their coffee, a new customer walked into the diner, Grayson Bennett himself, looking slightly sheepish but determined as he made his way toward the counter. Ruby greeted him with a knowing smile, but she kept her comments to herself, instead pouring him a fresh cup of coffee.

"Morning, Grayson. How'd you sleep after all the excitement last night?"

Grayson accepted the coffee with a grateful nod, though he couldn't quite meet her eyes. "Morning, Ruby. I slept fine, thanks. Just, uh, trying to get used to all the attention, I guess."

Ruby chuckled, leaning on the counter as she gave him a sympathetic look. "You'll get used to it, don't worry. The town's just excited about a little romance. It's been a while since we had something to talk about besides corn prices and bingo night."

Grayson sighed, taking a sip of his coffee. "I just don't want Evie to feel overwhelmed, you know? She's not used to all this... attention."

Ruby's smile softened, and she gave him a reassuring pat on the arm. "Evie's tougher than you think, Grayson. She'll be fine. And besides, she's got you looking out for her, doesn't she?"

Grayson's ears turned a little pink, but he managed a small smile. "Yeah, I guess she does."

Ruby winked, straightening up as the bell over the door jingled again. "Well, you just make sure she knows that, okay? Now go on, before those ladies in the corner rope you into telling them your whole life story."

Grayson chuckled, offering Ruby a grateful nod before heading for the exit, but as he passed Miss Pearl's table, he couldn't help but overhear a snippet of their conversation.

"Oh, he's smitten, all right," Betty was saying, her voice carrying clearly through the diner. "You can see it in the way he looks at her."

Grayson's face burned, but he forced himself to keep walking, pretending not to hear. He knew better than to try and argue with the town's gossip mill, especially when, deep down, he wasn't entirely sure they were wrong.

※

Back at Iris & Ivy, the morning rush was just beginning to pick up, and Evie was doing her best to focus on the steady flow of customers rather than the persistent buzz of whispers that followed her wherever she went. But it was impossible to ignore the curious glances and the not-so-subtle questions from her regulars.

"Did you have a nice time at the dance, Miss Evie?" asked Gary, the barber, as he paid for his bouquet of daisies. "I heard it was quite the night."

Evie forced a smile, handing him his change. "It was... nice, thank you, Gary."

Gary winked, tipping his hat before heading for the door. "Well, you just keep on having nice nights, all right?"

As the door closed behind him, Evie let out a long, exasperated sigh, dropping her head onto the counter. "I'm never going to hear the end of this, am I?"

Clara, who had returned with a fresh batch of muffins from Helen's bakery, patted her on the back with a grin. "Nope. But look on the bright side, at least it's not another haunted closet."

Evie couldn't help but laugh at that, lifting her head and shaking it. "I suppose that's true. I think I'll take overblown gossip over mysterious noises any day."

Clara leaned in closer, her grin turning sly. "Besides, Evie, you have to admit, there's something kind of... romantic about all this. A handsome neighbor sweeping you off your feet, a kiss under the stars... it's like something out of one of those old black-and-white movies."

Evie rolled her eyes but couldn't quite hide the small, shy smile that tugged at the corners of her lips. "You're as bad as Miss Pearl, you know that?"

Clara shrugged, unbothered. "I'll take that as a compliment. And speaking of Miss Pearl, I ran into her this morning on my way over. She wants you to stop by the diner for lunch. Said she had something important to discuss with you."

Evie groaned, rubbing her temples. "Let me guess, more matchmaking advice?"

Clara's smile softened, and she nudged Evie playfully. "Maybe. But don't worry, I think she means well. And I'm sure Grayson does too. Just... keep an open mind, okay?"

Evie nodded, though a part of her still felt wary about the whole situation. It was one thing to enjoy a dance and a sweet kiss, but she wasn't sure if she was ready for the pressure of the town's expectations, or the possibility of something more with Grayson. She had only just begun to find her footing in Magnolia Springs, and the idea of getting swept up in a whirlwind romance was as exciting as it was terrifying.

Lunchtime arrived faster than Evie expected, and she found herself standing outside Ruby's Diner, taking a deep breath before pushing open the door. The bell chimed overhead, and she braced herself for the inevitable wave of attention.

Sure enough, as soon as she stepped inside, heads turned, and conversations dropped to murmurs. Evie tried to ignore the curious stares, focusing instead on Miss Pearl, who waved her over to the booth by the window. Ruby, standing behind the counter, gave Evie a sympathetic smile before pouring her a fresh cup of coffee.

"Hello, dear!" Miss Pearl chirped, gesturing to the empty seat across from her. "Come sit down, Evie. We've got a lot to talk about."

Evie slid into the booth, eyeing Miss Pearl warily. "I don't know if I can handle more matchmaking schemes today, Miss Pearl."

Miss Pearl laughed, patting Evie's hand. "Oh, don't you worry, dear. Today isn't about schemes. Well, not *entirely*. I just wanted to see how you were holding up, with all the attention and all."

Evie let out a long sigh, leaning back in her seat. "Honestly, Miss Pearl, I'm not sure I'm cut out for being the center of town gossip. I moved here to get a fresh start, not to become the subject of every conversation."

Miss Pearl's expression softened, and for a moment, the playful mischief in her eyes gave way to genuine concern. "I know, Evie. And I'm sorry if we got a little carried away. But you have to understand, this town... well, we're a close-knit bunch. We don't get a lot of new faces, and when we do, we just want them to feel like they belong."

Evie nodded slowly, her frustration easing. She could see the sincerity in Miss Pearl's eyes, and she knew that beneath the meddling and the gossip, there was a genuine desire to make her feel at home. "I appreciate that, Miss Pearl. I really do. It's just... it's a lot to take in all at once."

Miss Pearl reached out, giving Evie's hand a reassuring squeeze. "I understand, dear. And if you ever need us to back off, you just say the word. But I have a feeling that you and Grayson might just surprise each other, and maybe even yourselves."

Evie managed a small smile, glancing out the window at the town square where the magnolia tree stood tall and proud. "Yeah, maybe."

Before Miss Pearl could respond, the doorbell jingled again, and Evie turned to see Grayson walking in. He looked a little taken aback to see her there but quickly recovered, offering her a warm smile as he approached the booth.

"Hey, Evie. Miss Pearl," he greeted, giving the older woman a polite nod before turning back to Evie. "Mind if I join you?"

Evie's heart skipped a beat, but she kept her voice steady. "Sure, Grayson. We were just... talking."

Grayson slid into the booth beside Miss Pearl, his expression curious. "I hope you're not plotting anything too dangerous, Miss Pearl."

Miss Pearl let out a laugh, patting Grayson's arm. "Oh, you know me, Grayson, just a harmless little chat between friends. But I'll leave you two to it. I've got to go check on my friends and see if they need any more... guidance."

She winked at Evie before slipping out of the booth, leaving the two of them alone. Evie watched her go, a mix of amusement and exasperation bubbling up inside her. She turned back to Grayson, who was looking at her with that same warm, slightly shy smile she'd come to recognize.

"So," he said, his voice low enough that it felt like they had their own private space despite the bustling diner around them. "How's your morning been? Surviving all the attention?"

Evie let out a rueful laugh, leaning forward on her elbows. "Barely. I didn't realize a dance could cause such a stir."

Grayson rubbed the back of his neck, a sheepish grin tugging at his lips. "Yeah, I guess I should've warned you. This town has a way of making a big deal out of... well, everything."

Evie shook her head, but she couldn't help the smile that softened her expression. "It's okay. I guess I'm just not used to being the center of attention. But... thank you for last night. I really did have a good time."

Grayson's smile grew, and he reached across the table, brushing his fingers lightly over the back of her hand. "I'm glad, Evie. I did too."

For a moment, the bustling diner seemed to fade away, leaving just the two of them and the warmth of their shared smile. Evie felt the tension in her chest ease, the worries and uncertainties of the morning slipping away like mist under the sun.

But then the bell above the door jingled again, and Ruby's voice called out from behind the counter. "Well, if it isn't Mrs. Jackson! Here to get the latest scoop, I see!"

Evie turned to see Mrs. Jackson, the town's most notorious gossip, sauntering into the diner with a gleam in her eye. She was a petite woman with a perfectly coiffed bob of silver hair and a nose for scandal that rivaled a bloodhound's. She spotted Evie and Grayson immediately, and her smile turned sharp with interest.

"Well, good morning, Evie, Grayson," Mrs. Jackson said, sidling up to their booth with the air of someone who'd stumbled upon a treasure trove of juicy information. "I hear you two had quite the night at the dance!"

Evie barely resisted the urge to groan, but Grayson gave Mrs. Jackson a polite smile, clearly more accustomed to handling her nosy ways. "Morning, Mrs. Jackson. We had a nice time, yes. But you know how it is, just a couple of neighbors enjoying the evening."

Mrs. Jackson's eyes sparkled with mischief. "Oh, I'm sure. And that little kiss at the end of the night, was that just neighborly too?"

Evie felt her face heat up, but before she could respond, Grayson's expression turned surprisingly serious. He met Mrs. Jackson's gaze head-on, his voice firm but good-natured. "It was exactly what it looked like, Mrs. Jackson, just a goodnight kiss between friends. And I'd appreciate it if you'd let the town know that."

Mrs. Jackson blinked, clearly caught off guard by Grayson's directness, but she quickly recovered, her smile turning more genuine. "Well, I suppose I can't argue with that. But you know us, Grayson, we can't resist a good story."

Grayson's expression softened, and he glanced at Evie, his smile turning warmer. "Yeah, I know. But sometimes, it's nice to let things happen in their own time, don't you think?"

Mrs. Jackson studied him for a moment, then nodded, a hint of respect in her eyes. "You've got a point, Grayson. Maybe we could all use a little more patience."

With that, she waved goodbye and headed for the counter, leaving Evie and Grayson alone again. Evie let out a breath she hadn't realized she was holding, turning to Grayson with a grateful smile. "Thank you for that. I'm not sure I could've handled another round of questions."

Grayson chuckled, reaching out to brush a stray curl behind her ear. "Anytime, Evie. I told you, I'm here for you, whatever you need."

Evie's heart gave a little flutter at the gentle touch, and for the first time that day, she felt a genuine sense of hope. Maybe the gossip would fade, and maybe it wouldn't, but she knew one thing for sure, she wasn't facing it alone.

And as she sat there with Grayson, surrounded by the warmth and chaos of Magnolia Springs, she realized that maybe that was enough.

Chapter 12

The bell above Iris & Ivy's door jingled as Evie rearranged a new display of autumn bouquets, the warm scent of roses and chrysanthemums filling the air. She turned, expecting to see a familiar face, but instead, a young woman in her early twenties stepped inside, her long brown hair pulled back into a high ponytail that swayed as she moved. She wore a casual sweater and jeans, and her wide, curious eyes took in the shop's displays with a kind of shy wonder.

"Hi there, welcome to Iris & Ivy," Evie greeted, offering the newcomer a friendly smile. "Can I help you with anything today?"

The young woman hesitated near the door, tucking a strand of hair behind her ear. "Oh, um, I'm just looking, thanks. Clara said I should check out your shop. She's a good friend, she wouldn't stop talking about how nice you are."

Evie's smile widened with recognition. "You must be Sadie, then. Clara's mentioned you a few times. She didn't say you'd be coming to visit, though."

Sadie's cheeks turned a faint pink, and she ducked her head shyly. "Yeah, I'm Sadie Williams. I run the Williams General Store for my parents."

Evie's expression softened with understanding, and she motioned for Sadie to come closer. "Well, I'm glad you stopped by. Clara's a great friend, and if she says you're good people, then I trust her judgment. How about I put together a little bouquet for you? You can put it on the counter at the general store."

Sadie's eyes brightened, and she took a tentative step forward, her fingers fiddling with the hem of her sweater. "That's really sweet of you, Evie. Thank you. I try to meet new people in town, but I'm terrible shy and it's hard for me, you know?"

Evie nodded, selecting a few flowers from the display as she spoke. "I get it."

Sadie laughed, the sound soft but genuine. "Everyone here are really nice. But they can be a little overwhelming."

"Yeah, they can be, but their heart is in the right place. Evie finished tying the bouquet with a bright ribbon and handed it to Sadie. "Here you go. And don't be a stranger, okay? If you ever need someone to talk to or just a place to escape to for a while, Iris & Ivy is always open to you."

Sadie's smile was small but sincere, and she clutched the bouquet to her chest like a lifeline. "Thank you, Evie. That means a lot. Really."

The bell jingled again, signaling another arrival, and both women turned to see a tall, slightly awkward-looking man with sandy blond hair step inside. He looked to be in his late twenties, with a lean build and a pair of glasses perched on the bridge of his nose. He wore a plaid shirt tucked into well-worn jeans, and his expression was caught somewhere between determination and uncertainty as he spotted Sadie standing by the counter.

"Uh, hey, Sadie," he said, offering her a hesitant smile. "I... didn't expect to see you here."

Sadie's cheeks turned even pinker, and she tucked her hair behind her ear again, giving him a small, shy wave. "Hi, Wyatt. Yeah, um, I was just... looking around."

Evie watched the interaction with quiet curiosity, sensing the awkward tension between the two of them. She couldn't help but notice the way Sadie's gaze lingered on Wyatt, or the way Wyatt seemed to fidget with his hands when he looked at her.

"Well, you're just in time, Wyatt," Evie said, stepping in to ease the silence. "I was just getting to know Sadie. Are you two friends?"

Wyatt cleared his throat, glancing at Sadie before looking back at Evie. "Um, yeah, I guess you could say that. I mean, we've, uh, seen each other around town a bit."

Sadie's blush deepened, but she shyly smiled at Wyatt.

Evie hid a smile behind her hand, charmed by the awkward dance between the two of them. She could tell that there was a connection there, even if neither of them seemed quite ready to admit it. "Wyatt, did you need some flowers for some one?"

Wyatt chuckled nervously, running a hand through his tousled hair. "Yes, my mom's birthday is tomorrow and I wanted to buy her a nice plant for her kitchen." Thanks, Evie."

There was another beat of silence, and then Sadie cleared her throat, clutching the bouquet a little tighter. "I, um, should probably get going. I got to get back to the store. Thank you again, Evie. And... I'll see you around, Wyatt?"

Wyatt nodded, a shy smile tugging at the corners of his mouth. "Yeah, definitely. See you around, Sadie."

Sadie offered one last smile before turning and heading for the door, the bouquet cradled in her arms. Wyatt watched her go, his expression thoughtful and a little wistful, and Evie couldn't resist the urge to tease him just a bit.

"She seems nice." Evie remarked casually, turning to pick out a nice calla lily plant for Wyatt's mother.

Wyatt cleared his throat, shuffling his feet awkwardly. "Yeah, she's, um, she's really nice. I just... I don't want to make things weird, you know? I mean, she already gets really nervous around me, and I don't want to come on too strong or anything."

Evie sat the plant on the counter and raised an eyebrow, giving him a knowing smile. "You know, Wyatt, some people don't know what to do with feeling they are feeling towards someone. They get quiet, act nervous," She gave him a pointed look. Sometimes it takes time and communication to overcome the awkwardness."

Wyatt looked down, scuffing his boot against the floor. "Yeah, maybe you're right. It's just... been a while since I've tried to get to know someone like that. I feel kind of... rusty, I guess."

Evie softened at his words, recognizing the uncertainty in his voice. "Well, for what it's worth, Wyatt, I think you're doing just fine. And if you ever need advice, you know where to find me too."

Wyatt looked up, a grateful smile crossing his face. "Thanks, Evie. I appreciate that. And... good luck with all the gossip about you and Grayson. Sounds like it's been a wild ride."

Evie laughed, shaking her head. "Oh, you have no idea. But I think I'm starting to get the hang of it. Just take things one step at a time, right?"

Wyatt nodded, giving her a small, genuine smile before heading for the door. "Yeah. One step at a time."

As the bell jingled again and the door swung shut behind him, Evie watched him walk down the street, catching up with Sadie as she made her way toward the general store. She saw the way they fell into step beside each other, talking quietly, and she couldn't help but hope that maybe they'd find a little bit of what she was starting to find with Grayson, a connection, a chance to build something new.

And as she returned to her flowers, the morning sun streaming through the shop windows, Evie realized that Magnolia Springs had a way of bringing people together, even in the most unexpected ways. Maybe, just maybe, Sadie and Wyatt were about to discover that for themselves.

Chapter 13

The living room of Miss Pearl's cozy cottage buzzed with energy as the Match Making Club convened for their latest meeting. Sunlight streamed through lace curtains, casting dappled patterns on the worn floral rugs, while the warm, homey scent of cinnamon cookies, Ruby's latest batch, filled the air. The familiar scene was set: Betty in the armchair near the window, wearing her favorite pink cardigan and clutching her knitting needles; Ruby perched on the loveseat with her tea, her curly hair slightly frizzed from the humid autumn air; and Hattie rocking gently in the old wicker chair by the fireplace, her glasses perched on the end of her nose as she peered at Miss Pearl with curiosity.

Miss Pearl herself, the ringleader of this mischievous quartet, stood before them with an air of importance, her hands clasped behind her back. She wore a dress patterned with tiny roses, her silver hair pinned up neatly. Her face bore a look of determination, tempered with a touch of frustration.

"Ladies, we need to talk about Evie and Grayson," she announced, her voice firm with a hint of exasperation.

Betty raised an eyebrow as she looped her yarn into neat stitches. "Why, what's wrong, Pearl? They danced together at the church event, and Grayson even kissed her goodnight. The town's been buzzing about it for weeks."

Ruby nodded in agreement, her lips curving into a sly smile. "And let me tell you, they've given folks plenty to talk about. I swear, I've served more slices of 'Kiss of the Century' pie these last few weeks than I did during the whole summer."

Miss Pearl waved a hand dismissively, though she couldn't help but smile at Ruby's mention of the pie. "Yes, yes, that part went just fine. But that was weeks ago, and since then? Nothing. They're dragging their feet, and I'm not about to let them waste the perfect chance we gave them."

Hattie, always the practical one, adjusted her glasses and leaned forward. "So, what do you have in mind this time, Pearl? We need something that'll really give them a nudge, something they can't just dance their way out of."

Miss Pearl's expression turned sly, and she lowered her voice, glancing around the room as if they were planning a heist. "Well, I've been thinking... What if we arrange a little *retreat* for them? A weekend up at Betty's cousin's old cabin by the lake. It's secluded, it's cozy, and it's got just enough charm to make even the most stubborn hearts melt."

Betty nearly dropped her knitting, her eyes going wide. "Pearl, you can't be serious! You want to *trap* them in a cabin together?"

Miss Pearl raised a finger, correcting her with a smile. "Not trap, dear—*encourage*. Evie's been talking about gathering fall wildflowers for some new arrangements at the shop, hasn't she? We'll teaser her with swamp sunflowers and cardinal flowers. And Grayson's always looking for an excuse to play the hero. We'll just suggest to Evie that she could use a little help up there, and then we'll let Grayson know she's planning to go. A cozy cabin, a little rain, and voila!"

Ruby's eyes lit up with understanding, and she set her teacup down with a soft clink. "Oh, I see what you're getting at. They'll be up there alone, surrounded by nature, with no one else around to distract them. They'll have no choice but to get to know each other better."

Hattie chuckled, clapping her hands together. "And if the weather forecast just so happens to call for a little rain, well, they might find themselves holed up by the fireplace. Nothing like a storm to bring two people closer."

Betty, who had been skeptical at first, couldn't help but smile at the thought of Evie and Grayson sitting by a crackling fire, perhaps sharing stories, or more. "You know, Pearl, you might just be onto something. But what if they don't go along with it? What if Grayson's too shy to make a move?"

Miss Pearl's eyes twinkled with a mixture of mischief and determination. "Oh, don't you worry about that. I'll make sure Grayson knows how much Evie could use a strong, capable man like him up there. And I'll plant the idea in Evie's mind that she might need a little assistance, just in case she runs into a wild animal or two."

Ruby laughed, shaking her head. "You're devious, Pearl. But I like it."

Hattie rocked back in her chair, her smile widening. "Well, while we're on the subject of matchmaking, I've got a suggestion for our next project."

Miss Pearl raised an eyebrow, intrigued. "Oh? Who do you have in mind, Hattie?"

Hattie's grin turned almost conspiratorial, and she glanced around the room before speaking. "Sadie and Wyatt."

Betty and Ruby exchanged curious glances, while Miss Pearl considered Hattie's words with a thoughtful nod. "You mean Clara's friend Sadie, the shy little thing who's been working at Ruby's Diner? And Wyatt Hawkins?"

Hattie nodded enthusiastically, her eyes shining. "That's right. I've seen the way they look at each other when they think no one's watching. They're as skittish as a pair of kittens, but there's definitely something there. If we don't step in, they'll be tiptoeing around each other for months."

Ruby leaned back, a thoughtful expression on her face. "You know, I think you're right, Hattie. Sadie's sweet, but she's got no idea how to make the first move. And Wyatt... well, he's a good man, but he's shy as a church mouse when it comes to women."

Betty set down her knitting, crossing her arms with a knowing smile. "Sounds like a challenge, all right. But I think it could be fun, after we get Evie and Grayson sorted, of course."

Miss Pearl couldn't help but smile at the enthusiasm of her friends, feeling a renewed sense of excitement for the possibilities ahead. "I like it, ladies. But let's focus on one project at a time. First, we get Evie and Grayson up to that cabin, and then we'll start working on bringing Sadie and Wyatt together."

She clapped her hands, signaling the end of their meeting. "Now, let's get to work. Betty, you make sure the cabin's ready and stocked with all the essentials. Ruby, I'll need you to spread a few hints around town about how lovely the wildflowers are up by the lake this time of year. And Hattie, I'll leave it to you to make sure Grayson hears about Evie's little trip. Let's give them the push they need."

The women shared a conspiratorial smile, their laughter mingling with the sound of the ticking grandfather clock in the corner of the room. They knew they were meddling, perhaps more than they should, but they also knew that sometimes love needed a little nudge in the right direction.

As the meeting wrapped up, Miss Pearl walked her friends to the door, each of them stepping out into the cool autumn evening with their baskets and bags. The sun was beginning to set, casting a warm glow over the town, and Miss Pearl couldn't help but feel a thrill of anticipation as she imagined how her plan would unfold.

She stood on her porch for a moment longer, watching as her friends disappeared down the street, their voices fading into the night. Then she glanced back toward the lights of the town square, her thoughts turning to Evie and Grayson, and to the new project that awaited them with Sadie and Wyatt.

"I hope you're ready, Evie," she murmured to herself, a satisfied smile playing at the corners of her mouth. "Because your adventure is just beginning."

And with that, she turned and headed back inside, already planning the details of her next move. Little did she know, the winds of change were already stirring in Magnolia Springs, bringing with them the promise of new connections, unexpected romance, and more than a few surprises for the town's most dedicated matchmakers

Chapter 14

The sun dipped low over Magnolia Springs, casting a warm, rosy glow across the town square. Evening settled in like a soft blanket, and the lights from Ruby's Diner spilled out onto the sidewalk, inviting the night's diners with the promise of comfort food and friendly conversation. Inside, the clink of cutlery and the murmur of voices created a cozy atmosphere, and the scent of fried chicken and freshly baked rolls filled the air.

Evie and Grayson sat in a booth near the window, the air between them buzzed with an unspoken energy. Evie found herself sneaking glances at Grayson over the rim of her water glass. He looked handsome tonight, his dark hair slightly tousled, his blue button-up shirt bringing out the color of his eyes in a way that made her stomach flutter.

They'd spent the evening talking about everything and nothing, sharing stories from their childhoods, laughing over the town's quirks, and discussing the endless gossip that seemed to follow them wherever they went. But now, as they finished their meal and Ruby came by to clear their plates, Evie couldn't ignore the way her heart raced every time Grayson's hand brushed hers.

"Can I get you two anything else? Maybe a slice of Helen's famous pecan pie?" Ruby asked, her sharp eyes darting between them with a knowing smile.

Evie shook her head, her cheeks warming under Ruby's gaze. "No, I think we're good, Ruby. Thanks."

Grayson smiled up at Ruby, his hand resting casually on the table between them. "Yeah, thanks, Ruby. I think we'll just settle up and head out."

Ruby winked at Evie as she picked up the check. "All right, you two lovebirds enjoy the rest of your evening. And don't let Miss Pearl rope you into any more of her schemes, you hear?"

Evie laughed, though the mention of Miss Pearl sent a twinge of suspicion through her. "No promises, Ruby. You know how persuasive she can be."

Ruby's laughter followed them out the door as they stepped into the cool evening air. Grayson held the door open for Evie, and she couldn't help but smile at his old-fashioned manners. They walked side by side down the quiet street, the town square glowing softly under the streetlights.

As they approached Iris & Ivy, Grayson slowed his steps, his hand brushing against Evie's as they walked. Evie's heart beat faster, and she tried to focus on the familiar sight of her flower shop rather than the warmth of his presence beside her.

"Thank you for dinner, Grayson," she said, her voice a little breathless. "I had a really nice time tonight."

Grayson turned to face her, his expression softening as he looked down at her. "Me too, Evie. I always enjoy spending time with you."

They stopped in front of the shop's door, and for a moment, the night seemed to hold its breath around them. Grayson took a step closer, his hand reaching out to brush a stray curl behind her ear, and Evie's breath caught at the gentleness of the gesture.

"Evie, I—" he started, but then he hesitated, as if searching for the right words. His thumb brushed against her cheek, sending a shiver down her spine. "I'm really glad you moved to Magnolia Springs. I feel like... like things have gotten a little brighter around here since you showed up."

Evie's cheeks flushed, and she glanced down, overwhelmed by the sincerity in his voice. "That's sweet of you to say, Grayson. I feel... I feel the same way about you. You've made me feel like I belong here."

Grayson's smile widened, and he tilted her chin up gently, forcing her to meet his gaze. "You do belong here, Evie. And I'm... well, I'm really happy that you're giving me a chance to get to know you."

Before Evie could respond, Grayson leaned in, closing the distance between them in one smooth motion. His lips brushed against hers, soft and tentative at first, as if he was testing the waters. But when Evie responded, her hands reaching up to curl into the fabric of his shirt, her lips parting slightly in surprise, he deepened the kiss, pouring all the unspoken feelings that had been building between them into that single moment.

For Evie, time seemed to stop. The cool breeze of the night, the distant hum of the town, even the soft glow of the shop's windows, all of it faded into the background as Grayson's kiss sent warmth flooding through her, leaving her breathless and lightheaded. She hadn't realized how much she'd been wanting this until it happened, and now, she never wanted it to end.

When Grayson finally pulled back, he stayed close, his forehead resting gently against hers as they both caught their breath. Evie's heart pounded in her chest, and she couldn't help the smile that tugged at her lips as she looked up at him, seeing the same awe and wonder reflected in his eyes.

"That was... wow," she whispered, feeling a little dazed.

Grayson chuckled softly, his hand lingering against her cheek. "Yeah. Wow."

They stood like that for a moment longer, savoring the closeness, until a sudden sound from across the square broke the spell, a loud crash, followed by a familiar cackle of laughter. Evie turned, frowning in confusion as she spotted Miss Pearl and her friends hurriedly ducking behind the large magnolia tree in the town square.

"What on earth...?" Evie murmured, squinting at the shadows moving among the tree's low-hanging branches.

Grayson followed her gaze, his expression turning wry. "Looks like Miss Pearl's up to something again. Should we go find out what it is?"

Evie hesitated, glancing back at the flower shop. A part of her was curious, but another part of her wanted to hold onto this moment with Grayson, to stay wrapped up in the warmth of his arms a little while longer. But before she could make a decision, the door of Iris & Ivy creaked open behind them, caught by a stray breeze, and the scent of roses drifted out into the night.

Grayson squeezed her hand, giving her a soft, reassuring smile. "Go on inside, Evie. It's late, and you've had a long day. I'll take a look around, make sure there aren't any more... surprise visitors."

Evie bit her lip, then nodded, stepping back reluctantly. "Okay. But be careful, Grayson. And... thank you. For everything."

Grayson bent down and gave her another quick kiss because he couldn't stop himself. Pulling back, he winked at her, the playful side of him she was beginning to adore showing through. "You don't have to thank me, Evie. I'm just looking out for my favorite florist."

After one last quick kiss, and lingering look, Grayson turned and walked toward the town square, his silhouette blending into the shadows of the magnolia tree. Evie watched him go, her heart still racing, before slipping inside the shop and closing the door behind her.

She leaned against the door, pressing her fingers to her lips, still feeling the warmth of Grayson's kiss tingling on her skin. Despite everything that had happened, she couldn't stop the smile that spread across her face. For the first time in a long time, she felt like she was exactly where she was meant to be.

In the shadows of the town square, Miss Pearl led her group of matchmakers back to her cozy cottage. Their laughter mingled with the rustling leaves of the magnolia tree as they congratulated each other on the success of the evening.

"I think we've got those two right where we want them," Ruby said, her voice bubbling with excitement. She adjusted her shawl against the cool night air, her face glowing with satisfaction. "Did you see how Grayson couldn't keep his eyes off her?"

Betty snorted, her knitting bag clutched under one arm as they made their way down the narrow path to Miss Pearl's front porch. "And Evie looked like she was about to float away on a cloud. If that kiss doesn't push them closer, I don't know what will."

Hattie, ever the practical one, tugged her sweater tighter around her shoulders and looked up at Miss Pearl with an expectant expression. "All right, Pearl, what's next? You said you had a plan for a little getaway up at Betty's cousin's cabin?"

Miss Pearl smiled, fishing a set of keys out of her pocket and holding them up with a flourish. "That's right, ladies. The cabin's all ready for a romantic weekend, and I've already planted the idea in Evie's head that she should gather some of those rare wildflowers up by the lake. I told her all about those beautiful Cardinal flower and the swamp sunflowers. I'll make sure Grayson hears about it, and if all goes well, they'll find themselves with a little extra time together in a cozy little hideaway."

Ruby clapped her hands together, her eyes sparkling with delight. "Oh, Pearl, you really are a mastermind. How do you think Grayson will react when he realizes he's been set up?"

Miss Pearl shrugged, her smile turning sly. "Well, they might figure it out eventually, but by the time they do, they'll already be too wrapped up in each other to mind. Sometimes, all a romance needs is a little nudge in the right direction."

Hattie let out a chuckle, shaking her head. "And if that nudge just so happens to be in the form of a cozy cabin and a little rainstorm, well, who's to complain?"

The women shared a laugh as they reached Miss Pearl's front porch, the glow from the porch light casting long shadows across the garden. They settled onto the wicker chairs, letting the night air cool their flushed faces, and toasted each other with a cup of tea.

But as their conversation drifted to quieter topics, Hattie's thoughts turned back to their next project, and she nudged Miss Pearl's shoulder gently. "So, after we get Evie and Grayson all sorted, do you think it's time we give Sadie and Wyatt a little attention? Those two are hopelessly shy, but I swear, I've never seen a pair that needs each other more."

Miss Pearl's expression softened, and she nodded slowly. "I think you're right, Hattie. Sadie's got a gentle heart, but she's so shy, bless her heart. And Wyatt... well, he's one of the good ones, even if he doesn't know how to say what he's feeling."

Betty leaned forward, her knitting forgotten in her lap as she added, "They need a chance, just like Evie and Grayson. And I think they're going to need more than just a nudge, they'll need a full-on shove."

Ruby grinned, her fingers tapping against the arm of her chair as she thought. "Oh, I've got a few ideas for those two. Maybe a little accidental pairing at the next town event. Or perhaps we 'lose' their names in the drawing for the pie-baking contest, force them to be partners."

Miss Pearl chuckled, raising her glass in a toast. "To Sadie and Wyatt, then. May their hearts find each other with a little help from Magnolia Springs' finest match makers."

The women clinked their cups together, the sound ringing through the quiet night like a promise. They knew that there were challenges ahead, missteps and misunderstandings, the kind that made for the best stories, but they were ready for whatever came next. After all, if there was one thing they'd learned over the years, it was that love had a way of surprising even the most seasoned matchmakers.

And as the night stretched on, filled with laughter and plans, Miss Pearl couldn't help but feel a thrill of anticipation for the adventures still to come. Because in a town like Magnolia Springs, where love stories unfolded under the glow of porch lights and whispers carried through the trees, there was always another romance waiting to blossom.

And she, Miss Pearl, intended to make sure it happened, no matter what it took.

⁂

Evie could still fill the warmth of Grayson's kiss lingered on her lips, making her feel like she was floating. She took a moment to compose herself, leaning against the door and letting out a deep breath. The evening had taken a turn she hadn't expected, but it was a turn that left her feeling lighter, as if the weight of all her uncertainties had lifted.

She crossed the shop floor, heading for the stairs that led to her apartment above the shop. But before she could reach the first step, a soft thud echoed from the back room, stopping her in her tracks. Her pulse quickened, and she glanced toward the darkened hallway that led to the storage area.

"Not tonight, please," she whispered to herself, half-expecting another round of mysterious noises or ghostly tricks. But when nothing else followed, she shook her head and forced herself to continue upstairs, deciding that whatever it was, it could wait until morning.

As she reached her cozy apartment, Evie couldn't help but steal one last glance out the window. She caught a glimpse of Grayson walking through the square, his confident stride illuminated by the glow of the streetlights. Even from a distance, he looked like he belonged, solid, steady, and so different from the whirlwind of emotions she felt inside. She watched until he disappeared around the corner, a small smile playing on her lips as she finally turned away from the window.

.

Chapter 15

The morning sun shone brightly over Magnolia Springs, casting a golden glow over the town square. Evie stood at the counter of Iris & Ivy, trimming the stems of fresh gerbera daisies, their vibrant colors bringing life to the shop. She hummed softly as she worked, unaware that just down the street, Miss Pearl and her friends were already putting the final touches on their next matchmaking scheme.

Across town, Miss Pearl's cozy kitchen buzzed with energy as the matchmakers gathered around the old oak table. Betty sipped her coffee, leaning back in her chair with a satisfied smile, while Ruby scrolling through the latest weather report she'd looked up on her cell phone's weather app. Hattie adjusted her glasses, peering at the list Miss Pearl had scribbled on a notepad.

"So, Pearl, let's hear it," Betty said, setting down her cup. "How exactly are we going to get Evie and Grayson up to that cabin together? It's not like we can just push them into a car and send them off."

Miss Pearl grinned, tapping her pen against the notepad. "Oh, I've got that part all figured out. Evie's still has been talking about gathering some of those rare wildflowers that grow up by the lake. She mentioned it to me just the other yesterday, so I might have... *gently suggested* that she make a weekend trip out of it."

Ruby chuckled, leaning forward with a mischievous glint in her eye. "And let me guess, you just so happened to suggest that Grayson might be able to help her carry all those flowers back and watch out for local wild life?"

Miss Pearl's grin widened. "Precisely. I told her that the lake trail can be a bit tricky, and it wouldn't hurt to have someone around who knows the area. And as for Grayson... well, Hattie, that's where you come in."

Hattie nodded, pulling a folded note from her pocket. "I'll leave him a little anonymous tip this morning, told him that Evie's planning to head up to the lake this weekend, and that it might be a good idea for him to tag along, you know, just in case she needs help with navigating the trails, wild life encounters or just helping her carry all those flowers."

Betty clapped her hands together, clearly pleased. "Oh, Pearl, you've really outdone yourself this time. A secluded cabin, a beautiful lake, and a whole weekend together... if that doesn't get them talking, I don't know what will." Then she snorted with laughter. "As far as wild life is concerned, the only wild life they will encounter is a random skunk or a possum... Oh and old man Ferguson's drunk mule, if he gets into the moonshine again."

Everyone busted out laughing at the memory of the last group trip up to the lake.

Miss Pearl's smile softened, and she glanced out the window, imagining how things might unfold. "Well, let's just hope they realize what's right in front of them before the weekends over. Now, Ruby, how's the weather looking?"

Ruby waved the weather report with a flourish. "We've got a pretty good sized rainstorm coming in tomorrow afternoon, should be just enough to keep them inside by the fire for a night or two. And if that doesn't bring them closer, I don't know what will."

The women exchanged knowing smiles, feeling the thrill of their plan coming together. They finished their coffee, tidied up the kitchen, and left Miss Pearl's house with a sense of excitement buzzing between them. The stage was set, and now all they had to do was wait for Evie and Grayson to play their parts.

That same afternoon, Grayson Bennett stood outside his shop, leaning against the doorframe as he read over the note he'd found tucked under his windshield wiper that morning. It was a simple note, written in neat, anonymous script, but its message was enough to set his mind spinning:

Heard Evie's headed up to the lake this weekend. She might need some help navigating those old trails and carrying all those flowers she's always talking about. I hope she doesn't have any wildlife encounters...

Grayson frowned, folding the note and slipping it into his jacket pocket. He knew better than to ignore a tip like this, it had Miss Pearl's fingerprints all over it, even if the handwriting didn't quite match. And as much as he wasn't one for meddling, he couldn't deny that the idea of spending more time with Evie sounded like a good one.

A few hours later, he found himself walking over to Iris & Ivy, his hands tucked into his pockets and his mind racing with possible excuses for showing up unannounced. But when he arrived, he found Evie standing on the front steps, a list in hand and a determined look on her face.

"Hey, Evie," he greeted, offering her a small smile. "What's all this? You look like you're planning something."

Evie glanced up, her surprise quickly melting into a smile. "Oh, hey, Grayson. I was just getting ready to head out tomorrow morning, up to the lake, actually. Miss Pearl mentioned that the wildflowers up there are still in full bloom, and I thought it might be a good chance to gather some for the shop."

Grayson's eyebrows lifted in what he hoped was a casual expression of interest, even though his heart did a little flip at the thought of joining her. "Up to the lake, huh? That's a bit of a trek, especially if you're planning to bring back a lot of flowers. You know, I've hiked that trail plenty of times. I could come with you, help carry some of the load if you'd like."

Evie hesitated, her gaze flicking to the shop's windows as if considering whether she should go it alone. But then she caught the genuine kindness in Grayson's eyes, and she found herself nodding before she could talk herself out of it.

"That... actually sounds nice, Grayson. I could use the company. And I wouldn't mind the help, either."

Grayson's smile widened, and he nodded, feeling a surge of excitement that he quickly tamped down. "Great. How about I pick you up around eight tomorrow morning?"

Evie agreed, a warm feeling spreading through her chest as she imagined the trip. She waved goodbye to Grayson as he headed back to his shop, but as soon as he was out of sight, she couldn't help but glance toward the town square, where Miss Pearl's shop stood in the distance.

She had a sneaking suspicion that the older woman had something to do with Grayson's sudden offer, but for once, she found herself not minding the interference. After all, a day at the lake with Grayson sounded like the perfect opportunity to figure out just where their connection might lead.

───※───

The next morning dawned bright and clear, with only a few wisps of clouds on the horizon. Grayson arrived right on time, and Evie joined him in his truck, feeling a flutter of nerves as they set out on the winding road toward the lake. The drive was filled with easy conversation and comfortable silence, both of them soaking in the beauty of the surrounding woods as they slowly made their way up the windy trail.

By late morning, they reached the cabin, an old but charming structure nestled among tall pines, overlooking the sparkling water of the lake. Wildflowers bloomed all along the edge of the clearing, their petals dancing in the breeze, and Evie couldn't help but let out a delighted gasp as she stepped out of the truck.

"Oh, Grayson, look at them," she exclaimed, rushing over to the flowers. "They're even more beautiful than I imagined."

Grayson followed her, smiling at the way her face lit up with excitement. "Yeah, they are. But we've got plenty of time to gather them. How about we get settled in the cabin first?"

Evie nodded, letting him lead her inside. The cabin was simple but cozy, with a stone fireplace, a well-loved couch in front of it. There was also small old farm house table with table with a two mismatched chairs, a small full sized bed tucked in the far corner of the cabin and a postage stamp sized kitchen with a sink and prep area. It smelled faintly of cedar, and as Evie glanced around, she couldn't help but think that it was the perfect place for a weekend retreat.

The weather had been unusually warm for late October and they spent the afternoon exploring the woods around the cabin, gathering wildflowers and chatting about everything from childhood memories to their hopes for the future. But by late afternoon, clouds began to roll in, and a cool wind rustled the treetops.

Grayson glanced up at the darkening sky, a small smile tugging at his lips. "Looks like we might get a little rain tonight. Good thing we've got the cabin, huh?"

Evie smiled back, feeling a little shiver of excitement at the thought of being tucked away in the cabin, just the two of them, with a storm raging outside. "Yeah, good thing."

As the first drops of rain began to fall, they hurried inside, bringing the wildflowers with them and setting them on the table. Grayson got a fire going in the fireplace, the warmth quickly filling the cabin, while Evie arranged the flowers in makeshift vases, their vibrant colors adding a touch of cheer to the space.

They settled in by the fire, sharing a quiet dinner of sandwiches, chips, and two sliced of triple chocolate cake that Ruby had packed for them as they listening to the sound of the rain pattering against the roof. The evening stretched on, filled with soft laughter and the gentle crackle of the flames, and Evie couldn't help but feel like she was exactly where she was meant to be.

Outside, hidden in the shadows of the woods, Miss Pearl smiled as she adjusted her raincoat, her heart swelling with satisfaction. Her plan had gone off without a hitch, and now it was up to Evie and Grayson to make the most of their time together.

"Good luck, you two," she whispered into the night, before carefully walking back to her car and driving back down the winding road toward town.

As the rain picked up, the gentle drizzle turning into a steady patter against the roof, Evie leaned back on the couch near the fire, letting the warmth of the flames soak into her skin. Grayson sat next to her, stretching his long legs toward the hearth. He stood and stoked the embers with a poker.

Outside, the world was reduced to a blur of mist and rain, the steady rhythm creating a peaceful backdrop to their evening. Evie glanced at Grayson, noticing the way the firelight cast shadows across his face, highlighting the strong line of his jaw and the easy smile that seemed to come more naturally to him these days.

"So, Grayson," Evie began, her voice breaking the comfortable silence, "how did you end up in Magnolia Springs? I mean, I know you've lived here a when you were younger, but I don't think I ever heard the whole story."

Grayson chuckled softly, leaning back in his chair. "Well, it's not as exciting as you might think. I was born and raised here. I moved away almost ten years ago, to go to college. After College, I lived in the

Atlanta area. I guess I just got tired of all the noise and chaos there. When my uncle messaged me and told me he was retiring, he gave me first shot at buying it his hardware store. After Atlanta, Magnolia Springs felt like a breath of fresh air, literally and figuratively."

Evie tilted her head, intrigued. "So you just picked up and moved?"

He shrugged, his smile turning a little wistful. "Yeah, pretty much. My sister, Maddie wasn't too thrilled about it at first, but she came around eventually. I worry about her being Atlanta all by herself, though. I'm trying to talk her into moving back here. I told her that once I settled in, I realized I missed the slower pace, the way people in this town actually care about each other. I told her it felt... it like home?"

Evie nodded, understanding the sentiment more than she'd expected. "I wasn't planning to stay here when I inherited the shop from my aunt Iris, but the town grew on me."

Grayson's expression softened as he met her gaze across the fire. "I'm glad you stayed, Evie. Magnolia Springs is better with you in it. I'm better with you in in it."

Evie's cheeks warmed, and she glanced away, pretending to focus on the fire. But she couldn't stop the small smile that tugged at her lips. There was something about Grayson that made her feel seen, like he understood her in a way that no one else had in a long time.

They fell into a comfortable silence again, the sound of the rain growing heavier as the storm rolled in. Outside, the wind began to howl, and the trees creaked and swayed under the force of the gusts. Evie shivered slightly, pulling her sweater closer around her shoulders.

Grayson noticed, and without a word, he got up to grab an extra blanket from the bed in the corner of the cabin. He draped it over her shoulders, his fingers brushing against her collarbone as he tucked it around her. The touch was brief, but it sent a spark of warmth through Evie that had nothing to do with the fire.

"Thank you," she murmured, looking up at him with a grateful smile.

Grayson returned to his seat, but his expression was more serious now, his gaze lingering on her as if he was trying to read her thoughts. "Evie, can I ask you something?"

She nodded, suddenly feeling a little nervous under the intensity of his gaze. "Of course, you can ask me anything. What's on your mind?"

He hesitated for a moment, then took a deep breath, as if gathering his courage. "Do you ever feel like... like maybe you're afraid to let yourself be happy? Like you keep holding back, even when there's something, someone, right in front of you who might make you happy?"

Evie's breath caught in her throat, and she felt her heart begin to race. It was as if Grayson had reached into her mind and pulled out the thoughts she'd been trying so hard to ignore. She met his eyes, seeing the vulnerability there, and realized that he wasn't just talking about her, he was talking about himself, too.

"I think... I think I know what you mean," she said softly, her fingers tightening around the edge of the blanket. "It's scary, isn't it? The idea of opening up to someone, of letting them see all the parts of you that you usually keep hidden."

Grayson nodded, his gaze never leaving hers. "Yeah, it is. But I think maybe... maybe it's worth the risk."

Evie swallowed hard, feeling the weight of his words settle deep inside her. For a long moment, they just looked at each other, the unspoken tension between them crackling like the fire that warmed the room. And then, slowly, Evie reached out, her hand trembling slightly as she placed it over his.

"I think you might be right, Grayson," she whispered, her voice barely more than a breath. "Maybe it is worth it."

Grayson's hand turned, his fingers curling around hers as he offered her a small, hopeful smile. "I'd like to find out, Evie. If you're willing to give me a chance."

Evie felt a lump rise in her throat, but she forced herself to smile back, feeling a sense of certainty settle in her chest. "I think I'd like that too, Grayson."

For a moment, the world outside disappeared, leaving just the two of them and the warmth of the fire that seemed to mirror the warmth growing between them. But then a loud crack of thunder split the air, making Evie jump in surprise. The lightening flashed in the small cabin lighting it up for just a second, then cabin was back to being lite by the glow of the fire.

Grayson let out a low laugh, reaching into his jacket pocket to retrieve a flashlight. "Looks like I need to get a few of those candle we brought with us lite before one of us trips over something. We're in for a long stormy night, Evie. But don't worry, I'm not going anywhere."

Evie chuckled, the sound a little shaky as she tried to steady her racing heart. "I guess we're going to have to rough it, aren't we?" she said with a hint of a smile tugging on her lips

Grayson turned on the flashlight, its beam cutting through the shadows, and gave her a reassuring smile. "Yeah. But you know what? I don't think I mind one bit."

After lighting a half a dozen candles, they settled back on the couch in front of the fire, sharing the blanket and the warmth of their newfound understanding, Evie couldn't help but feel like maybe, just maybe, this was the beginning of something real. Something that had been worth waiting for, even if she hadn't known it at the time.

Grayson's arm slipped around Evie's shoulders, pulling her closer until she was resting against his chest, listening to the steady beat of his heart. They talked late into the night, sharing stories and laughter, as they learned anymore about each other. The stormed raged on outside, but inside the cabin, they found a warmth that went beyond the crackling flames, a warmth that spoke of possibilities, of the chance to build something new.

And as Evie drifted off to sleep against Grayson's shoulder, she couldn't help but think that maybe, just maybe, this weekend would be the start of something that neither of them would ever forget.

Chapter 16

The storm had raged throughout the night, the rain drumming steadily against the cabin's roof, and the wind howling through the trees like a restless spirit. But inside, the warmth of the fire and the gentle glow of its embers had wrapped Evie and Grayson in a cocoon of comfort. They'd fallen asleep side by side on the small bed, wrapped in a shared blanket, with Evie nestled against Grayson's chest, lulled by the rhythmic beat of his heart.

But as dawn approached, the storm seemed to reach a new peak, the sky outside darkening once more as the wind picked up, rattling the cabin's old windowpanes. Suddenly, a tremendous clap of thunder split the air, shaking the very walls of the cabin and jolting Evie from sleep.

With a startled gasp, she clutched at Grayson's shirt, her arms wrapping around his neck instinctively as her breath came in quick, panicked bursts. "Grayson—"

Grayson woke with a start, his arms tightening around her, his senses coming alive as the storm raged outside. He glanced down at Evie, seeing the fear in her wide eyes, and reached up to brush a stray lock of hair from her face, his thumb lingering against her cheek.

"Its okay, Evie," he murmured, his voice rough with sleep but full of reassurance. "It's just the storm. I've got you."

But as their eyes met, something shifted between them, something deeper than the fear that had gripped Evie in that moment. Her pulse still raced, but now it wasn't just from the thunder. It was from the way Grayson's gaze softened as he looked at her, the way his hand cradled her cheek as if she were something precious.

And in that heartbeat of silence between them, the air seemed to thicken with unspoken words and unacknowledged feelings. Grayson's breath hitched, his eyes darkening as he took in the way Evie's lips parted slightly, the flush that spread across her cheeks.

Before he could second-guess himself, before he could let the weight of caution hold him back, he leaned down, his lips hovering just above hers. "Evie, I—"

But whatever he was about to say was lost as Evie closed the distance between them, her lips pressing softly against his. It was a tentative kiss at first, but then Grayson responded, pouring all of the longing and desire that had been building inside him into that single moment. His hand slid from her cheek to the back of her neck, pulling her closer as their kiss deepened, as if they were both trying to make up for all the time they'd spent holding back.

Evie's hands tightened in his shirt, pulling him closer as the fire that had simmered between them finally ignited, burning away any remaining doubts. The world outside, the thunder, the rain, the wind, disappeared, leaving only the heat of their kiss and the feeling of Grayson's arms around her, anchoring her to this moment.

When they finally broke apart, both of them were breathless, their foreheads pressed together as they struggled to catch their breath. Evie looked up at Grayson, her eyes wide with a mixture of surprise and something deeper, something she couldn't quite name but that made her heart ache with a fierce, unfamiliar longing.

"Grayson..." she whispered, her voice barely more than a breath.

But Grayson silenced her with another kiss, gentler this time, but no less intense. "I've wanted this for so long, Evie," he confessed, his voice rough with emotion. "I can't keep pretending that I don't feel an overwhelming need for this, for *you*."

Evie's heart swelled at his words, and she reached up to cup his face, her thumbs brushing against the rough stubble of his jaw. "Then don't deny it, Grayson," she whispered back, her voice trembling with the weight of everything she felt. "Don't hold back. Not anymore."

And with those words, the last of their restraint shattered. Grayson kissed her again, pouring all of his passion, his need, into the embrace, and Evie responded in kind, letting herself be swept away by the tide of emotions she'd been too afraid to acknowledge before. The blanket slipped to the floor as they gave in to the pull between them, finding solace in each other as the storm continued to rage outside.

The next morning, the storm had passed, leaving a misty calm that hovered over the lake, turning the water into a silver mirror that reflected the pale light of dawn. Inside the cabin, the fire had burned down to embers, but the warmth that filled the space remained, lingering in the air like the memory of a dream.

Evie woke slowly, the soft morning light filtering through the window and casting a gentle glow over the room. She shifted under the covers, feeling the warmth of Grayson's naked body beside her, and a sleepy smile tugged at her lips as she remembered the events of the night before.

She turned her head to find Grayson watching her, his blue eyes filled with a tenderness that made her heart skip a beat. He reached out, brushing his fingers lightly against her cheek, and Evie leaned into the touch, feeling a sense of peace settle over her that she hadn't known she was missing.

"Morning," he said softly, his voice still rough with sleep.

Evie's smile widened, and she reached up to trace the curve of his jaw with her fingertips. "Morning. How long have you been awake?"

Grayson shrugged, a lazy smile playing at his lips. "Long enough to realize that I don't want this weekend to end."

Evie's heart swelled at his words, and she leaned in to press a soft kiss to the corner of his mouth, savoring the way he responded instantly, as if he couldn't get enough of her. "Me neither," she admitted, her voice barely more than a whisper. "But I suppose we can't hide away up here forever."

Grayson chuckled, "we can try." but there was a hint of reluctance in the sound. "Yeah, I know, you're right. We should probably get packed up before the road back gets too muddy from the rain."

They reluctantly pulled themselves out of the warmth of the bed, getting dressed and gathering their things as the cabin filled with the soft sounds of morning, birds calling from the trees, the gentle rustle of leaves in the breeze, and the occasional crackle from the last embers in the fireplace.

But even as they packed their bags and tidied up the cabin, they couldn't seem to keep their hands from brushing against each other, their fingers lingering just a little too long as they passed a folded blanket or a basket of wildflowers. Every touch sent a spark through Evie's skin, and she couldn't help the way her smile kept slipping into something softer, something that hinted at the vulnerability she felt in this new, uncharted territory between them.

Grayson caught her around the waist as she reached for her bag, pulling her back against his chest and pressing a kiss to the top of her head. "You know, we could always come back here sometime," he murmured, his lips brushing against her hair. "Just the two of us."

Evie leaned into him, feeling the strength of his arms around her, and let out a contented sigh. "I'd like that, Grayson. I'd like that a lot."

He turned her gently in his arms, lifting her chin with his fingers until their eyes met. "Then let's make it happen, Evie. Let's stop pretending that we don't belong together."

Evie's breath caught at the determination in his voice, and she reached up to cup his face, her heart swelling with an emotion that felt too big to contain. "Okay," she whispered, her voice trembling. "Let's stop pretending."

Grayson's smile was slow and sweet, and he kissed her again, softly, lingeringly, as if sealing a promise between them. And when they finally pulled away, Evie knew that whatever came next, they would face it together.

They finished packing up the cabin, gathering two tote full of Cardinal flowers and swamp sunflowers. They loaded their things into the truck and taking one last look at the quiet, mist-covered lake, before they started the drive back to Magnolia Springs. The road was muddy from the rain, but Grayson handled it with ease, keeping one hand on the wheel and the other resting over Evie's, their fingers intertwined.

And as they left the cabin behind, the sun breaking through the clouds to cast a warm light over the countryside, Evie couldn't help but feel that they were stepping into something new, something real and honest, built on a foundation of shared smiles, whispered confessions, and the kind of connection she hadn't believed she'd ever find.

Whatever the future held, she knew that she wasn't facing it alone anymore. And that thought, more than anything, filled her with a sense of hope she hadn't felt in a long time.

As they drove back toward Magnolia Springs, the countryside seemed to bloom with new life in the aftermath of the storm. The sun broke through the clouds in golden rays, lighting up the mist that still lingered over the fields and creating a world that felt fresh and renewed, much like the feelings stirring between Evie and Grayson.

Evie watched the scenery pass by, a peaceful smile playing on her lips, her hand still resting in Grayson's. The warmth of his touch, the solid strength of his fingers entwined with hers, made her feel grounded in a way she hadn't realized she needed. She glanced sideways at him, taking in the relaxed lines of his face, the way his lips curved up slightly as he focused on the winding road ahead.

She had a thousand questions on her mind, questions about what their night together meant, about what might come next for them now that they had crossed a line neither of them could ignore. But every time she tried to form the words, she found herself holding back, not wanting to shatter the easy, comfortable silence that had settled between them.

Grayson seemed to sense her thoughts, because he glanced over, catching her eye with a small, reassuring smile. "You're awfully quiet over there, Evie. Everything okay?"

Evie let out a soft laugh, feeling a little self-conscious under his gaze. "Yeah, I'm okay. Better than okay, actually. I'm just... thinking."

Grayson's smile widened, and he squeezed her hand gently. "Thinking about last night?"

Evie's cheeks warmed, but she didn't look away this time. "Yeah. About last night, and... about what happens next, I guess."

Grayson's expression softened, and he brought her hand to his lips, pressing a tender kiss to her knuckles. "I've been thinking about that too," he admitted, his voice low and sincere. "And I want you to know, Evie, that whatever happens next, I'm in this for the long haul. I don't want this to just be some weekend fling."

Evie's heart swelled at his words, and she turned in her seat to face him fully, her voice trembling with the weight of what she wanted to say. "I don't want that either, Grayson. I've... I've been scared to open up to someone, to let myself feel like this. But with you, it feels... different. It feels like maybe I don't have to be so afraid anymore."

Grayson's grip on her hand tightened, and he glanced at her with an intensity that sent a shiver down her spine. "You don't have to be afraid, Evie. Not with me. I'm not going anywhere, and I'm not going to push you into anything you're not ready for. But I want to be with you, really be with you. And I want to see where this can go."

Evie's breath caught at the honesty in his voice, and she felt a lump rise in her throat, making it hard to speak. But she managed to smile through the emotion, her fingers tightening around his. "I want that too, Grayson. More than I ever thought I would."

They shared a look that spoke volumes, a look that carried all the unspoken promises and hopes that had been building between them since the day they'd met. And for the first time in a long time, Evie felt like she was stepping into something real, something that might last beyond the quiet mornings and stormy nights.

As the truck rounded the last bend, bringing the town of Magnolia Springs into view, Evie couldn't help but feel a flutter of anticipation. She knew that the path ahead wouldn't always be easy, that there would be challenges and misunderstandings, as there always were in matters of the heart. But with Grayson by her side, she felt ready to face whatever came next.

Grayson must have sensed her thoughts, because he leaned over and pressed a soft kiss to her lips, his voice gentle as he whispered, "Welcome home, Evie."

She smiled at the words, her heart warming at the realization that Magnolia Springs truly did feel like home now, because of the connections she'd made, because of the memories she'd created, and most of all, because of the man sitting beside her.

They pulled into the gravel driveway behind Iris & Ivy, the flower shop's windows glinting in the morning light. Grayson turned off the engine and helped Evie out of the truck, their hands lingering together as they carried her bag up to the back door of her flower shop.

When they reached the door with, Grayson set down the bag and turned to face her, his expression serious but filled with a quiet kind of joy. "Evie, I just want you to know... last night was the best night I've ever had. And I don't want it to be the last."

Evie's eyes softened, and she reached up to cup his face, brushing her thumb over the stubble on his cheek. "It won't be, Grayson. I promise."

He leaned down, capturing her lips in a kiss that was slow and sweet, a kiss that spoke of all the possibilities they'd only begun to explore. And when they finally pulled away, breathless and smiling, Evie couldn't help but feel like they were standing on the edge of something new and beautiful, something that neither of them had expected, but that felt right all the same.

Grayson gave her hand one last squeeze before stepping back, his eyes lingering on her as if he couldn't quite bring himself to leave. "I'll see you tonight, then? Dinner at my place?"

Evie nodded, a smile tugging at her lips. "Dinner at your place sounds perfect."

He grinned, leaning in for another quick peck on her lips before turning back toward his truck to retrieve her totes filled with wildflowers. "Great. I'll see you up at seven."

As he drove his truck to his own back parking area, Evie watched him go, feeling a warmth bloom in her chest that had nothing to do with the morning sun. And as she stepped inside the flower shop, breathing in the familiar scent of roses and greenery, she knew that whatever challenges lay ahead, she was ready to face them, because she wasn't facing them alone anymore.

<hr />

And somewhere in the heart of Magnolia Springs, Miss Pearl smiled as she watched from her store window, satisfied that her plan had brought yet another pair of hearts closer together. She knew there was still work to be done, new romances to encourage, new connections to nurture, but for now, she could rest easy, knowing that she'd helped Evie and Grayson find their way to each other.

With a contented sigh, Miss Pearl turned away from the window, already planning her next steps. After all, love didn't just bloom on its own, it needed a little help, a little encouragement, and sometimes, a well-timed thunderstorm.

Chapter 17

The sun shone brightly over Magnolia Springs on Monday morning, casting a warm golden glow over the sleepy town. The weekend's storm had given way to a crisp, clear day, with the air carrying the earthy scent of rain-soaked leaves. It was the kind of morning that made everything feel fresh and full of possibility, especially for Evie and Grayson.

Evie stood behind the counter of Iris & Ivy, her hands busy arranging a new display of chrysanthemums and autumn leaves. But no matter how hard she tried to focus on her work, she couldn't keep the smile from creeping across her face, and every time she thought about the weekend she'd shared with Grayson, a warm, giddy feeling bloomed in her chest.

She'd catch herself daydreaming about the way he'd looked at her when they were wrapped in each other's arms by the fire, or the way his laugh rumbled through his chest when they'd joked about their "mysterious" weekend getaway. And when she thought about the promises they'd made to each other, promises of something real, something lasting, her heart fluttered like a dozen butterflies had taken flight inside her.

But it wasn't just Evie who seemed to be floating on air that morning. Grayson had stopped by opening his hardware store, bringing her a cup of coffee and stealing a few quick kisses that left her cheeks flushed with pleasure. He'd left with a wink, his own smile as wide as the Magnolia River, and the knowing look in his eyes had made Evie's knees weak.

If they thought their happiness would go unnoticed in Magnolia Springs, however, they couldn't have been more wrong.

As soon as Grayson stepped out the door, Evie had caught sight of Helen from the bakery peering over Evie's display window, her eyes as round as saucers. Not ten minutes later, Ruby had strolled by with her morning paper, her smile a little too wide, and waved at Evie through the window.

And now, barely an hour after opening, Evie was stacking a fresh delivery of roses when she heard the shop's door fly open with a bang. She turned just in time to see Clara nearly skid across the wooden floor, her shoes squeaking against the polished boards as she rushed in, a whirlwind of energy and excitement.

"Evie!" Clara practically shrieked, her cheeks flushed pink with exertion. Her long, chestnut hair was half-tucked behind her ears, and her glasses had slipped down the bridge of her nose. She caught herself against the counter, trying to catch her breath but too excited to manage more than a few gasping words. "Oh my gosh, *is it true?* Did you and Grayson really, oh, you know, enjoy each other's company this weekend? And are you two, like, officially *official* now?"

Evie's eyes widened as her best friend launched into the question at ninety miles an hour, her words tumbling over each other like rocks in a river. Clara's excitement was contagious, but Evie couldn't help but feel her cheeks heat up as she realized just how much the town must have already heard. Clara's not-so-subtle wink only made the blush spread further, and Evie found herself fumbling for words.

"Clara! Keep your voice down!" Evie hissed, glancing toward the windows as if expecting the town's entire population to have their faces stuck to her front windows like a bunch of nosy gossiping Garfield cats as they eavesdropped. She shook her head, trying to hide her smile behind a strand of hair that had fallen loose from her braid. "And who told you that? We just got back last night!"

Clara rolled her eyes, leaning across the counter with a conspiratorial grin. "Oh, please, Evie, you know how fast news travels around here. I think half the town saw Grayson in your shop this morning, and you two looked like a couple of love-struck teenagers. You've both been grinning like the cat that got the cream."

Evie couldn't help but laugh, a mix of embarrassment and delight bubbling up inside her. She reached for a nearby rose and twirled it between her fingers, feeling like she was on the verge of a secret she wasn't quite ready to share, but not entirely willing to keep to herself, either. "Well, okay, maybe we *did* enjoy each other's company. And yes, I guess you could say we're officially together now. But, Clara, it's still new. We haven't even had a chance to—"

Clara let out a squeal of delight that could have rattled the windows, clapping her hands together like she'd just won the lottery. "I *knew* it! I *knew* you two had something special going on! Oh, this is so exciting, Evie! You have to tell me everything, I mean *everything*. What happened at the lake? Did he finally make a move? Was it romantic?"

Evie held up her hands, trying to calm her friend down before the entire shop filled with Clara's high-pitched enthusiasm. But despite her attempts at playing it cool, she couldn't keep the smile from her face as she thought back to the weekend. The way Grayson had held her close during the storm, the way he'd kissed her like she was the only thing that mattered in the world... it was more than she'd ever imagined for herself.

"It *was* romantic," she admitted, a soft, dreamy quality slipping into her voice despite herself. "Grayson was... well, he was amazing. He's so thoughtful, Clara, and he really made me feel like I could just... be myself. I've never felt that way with someone."

Clara's expression softened, and she reached out to squeeze Evie's hand, her eyes shining with genuine happiness. "I'm so happy for you, Evie. You deserve this, you deserve to be with someone who sees how amazing you are. And if Grayson's the one who can do that, then... well, I think he's a pretty lucky guy."

Evie's heart warmed at her friend's words, and she squeezed Clara's hand in return, feeling a swell of gratitude for having someone like her in her life. "Thank you, Clara. That means a lot, really. And... well, I'm happy too, happier than I've ever been."

Clara grinned, but her expression quickly turned mischievous, and she leaned in closer, lowering her voice to a whisper. "Okay, but you *have* to tell me, what was it like when you two finally, you know... *connected*? Was it everything you hoped for?"

Evie's cheeks went scarlet, and she glanced around the empty shop, making sure no one else had slipped inside while they were talking. "Clara! That's none of your business!"

Clara just waggled her eyebrows, clearly unrepentant. "Oh, come on, Evie, you can't blame a girl for being curious! Besides, the whole town is practically buzzing with questions. Might as well give me the inside scoop before everyone else starts making up their own stories."

Evie groaned, burying her face in her hands, but she couldn't help the laughter that escaped her. "You're impossible, you know that? Fine. It was... it was perfect, okay? More than perfect. But that's all you're getting out of me!"

Clara let out another delighted squeal, and for a moment, the two friends dissolved into laughter, the sound filling the flower shop with a warmth that matched the sunlight streaming through the windows. Evie felt a sense of relief wash over her as she shared this moment with Clara, knowing that, even though the gossip would fly, she had a friend who genuinely cared about her happiness.

Clara finally took a breath, her laughter tapering off as she straightened and gave Evie a more serious look, though a smile still lingered on her lips. "All joking aside, Evie, I'm really glad you've found someone like Grayson. It's about time you let yourself have a little happiness, you know?"

Evie nodded, feeling a lump rise in her throat. "Yeah. I think... I think I needed this. More than I realized. And I'm glad you're here to see it, Clara. Even if you are a nosy little thing."

Clara winked, clearly unoffended. "You know you love me, nosiness and all. And speaking of nosy, have you thought about what you're going to do about the town's questions? You know you're going to get a lot more of them today."

Evie sighed, glancing out the front window to where Miss Pearl's tea shop sat just across the square. She could almost see the older woman's silhouette behind the lace curtains, probably sipping her tea with a knowing smile. "Yeah, I know. I've already had a few curious looks this morning. I guess I can't keep everything a secret forever."

Clara gave her a gentle nudge, her expression turning sympathetic. "You don't have to spill all the details, Evie. Just give them enough to keep the rumors from getting too wild. And hey, if anyone gives you a hard time, just send them my way. I'll set them straight."

Evie laughed softly, feeling a little lighter at the thought. "I might just take you up on that, Clara. But I think I can handle it for now. It's just... new, you know? Grayson and I are still figuring things out, and I don't want everyone's opinions getting in the way."

Clara nodded, her expression softening with understanding. "I get it. And you're right, you should enjoy this time together. But just know, I'm rooting for you both. And I'll be here if you ever need to talk about... anything."

Evie smiled, feeling a wave of gratitude for Clara's friendship. "Thanks, Clara. You're the best."

Clara flashed her a grin, then glanced at the clock on the wall with a dramatic sigh. "Well, I guess I should get to work and let you get back to work before I scare off all your customers. But if you hear any more juicy gossip about your weekend, you *know* where to find me."

Evie rolled her eyes, but she couldn't help the laugh that bubbled up as Clara gave her a quick hug and then hurried out the door, practically skipping with excitement. As the door swung shut behind her, Evie took a deep breath, her smile lingering as she returned to her work.

But even as she arranged the last of the flowers, she couldn't ignore the flutter of nerves that settled in her stomach. Clara was right, people would be talking, and questions would keep coming. But for the first time, Evie felt like she might be ready to face it all, because she knew that no matter what happened, she had Grayson by her side.

The day passed in a blur of work, with Evie tending to her customers and managing the deliveries that arrived throughout the morning. But true to Clara's warning, she fielded a steady stream of curious glances and leading questions from the townspeople who came into the shop.

Helen from the bakery stopped by with a loaf of fresh bread, giving Evie a pointed look as she asked, "So, Evie, how was your weekend? Anything exciting happen up at the lake?"

Evie did her best to keep her tone casual as she accepted the bread with a smile. "It was nice, Helen. Very... relaxing. Grayson was kind enough to help me gather some wildflowers for the shop."

Helen's eyes twinkled with curiosity, but she just nodded, her smile widening. "Well, I'm glad to hear it, dear. You know, there's nothing like a little time away from town to help you see things clearly."

Evie thanked her for the bread, feeling a blush creep up her neck as she imagined what else Helen might have been implying. And by the time Miss Pearl herself strolled in later that afternoon, Evie was bracing herself for yet another round of hints and half-hidden smirks.

Miss Pearl, of course, was nothing if not direct. She leaned on the counter, her eyes sparkling with mischief as she surveyed Evie's carefully arranged displays. "Well, well, Evie, dear. Looks like you and Grayson had quite the time up at the cabin, hmm? I've been hearing all sorts of stories about the two of you. Care to share your side?"

Evie took a deep breath, forcing herself to meet Miss Pearl's gaze with a steady smile. "You know how people like to talk, Miss Pearl. But yes, Grayson and I did have a nice time. And I think... I think we're going to try and see where things go from here."

Miss Pearl's grin widened, and she reached out to pat Evie's hand, her voice warm with approval. "Well, it's about time, if you ask me. And just between you and me, I think the whole town is rooting for you two. It's always nice to see a good love story unfold."

Evie couldn't help but smile at the sincerity in Miss Pearl's words, even if she suspected the older woman had more than a little to do with the "stories" that had been circulating. "Thanks, Miss Pearl. I appreciate that. And... I appreciate the encouragement you've given me, even if it did come with a few surprises."

Miss Pearl chuckled, her eyes twinkling with a hint of mischief. "Oh, I'm sure I don't know what you're talking about, Evie. But I'll just say this, sometimes love needs a little nudge, and sometimes, well, it just needs a good old-fashioned shove."

They shared a laugh, and as Miss Pearl left the shop, Evie felt a sense of relief wash over her. Maybe things wouldn't be quite so simple now that everyone knew about her and Grayson, but she was starting to realize that she didn't mind the questions as much as she thought she would.

Because at the end of the day, she knew that the story she and Grayson were building together was worth every curious glance and every whispered word. And as she closed up the shop that evening, locking the door and stepping out into the cool dusk, she couldn't help but feel a sense of excitement for what the future might hold.

Next door, Grayson was dealing with his own share of gossip, though he handled it with the same easy charm that had always been his trademark. His regulars at the hardware store wasted no time in ribbing him about his weekend getaway, but Grayson took it in stride, a secretive smile never far from his lips.

"Well, Grayson," one of the older gentlemen drawled as he paid for a new set of tools, "word around town is that you and Evie Matthews have gotten mighty close lately. Anything you want to share with the rest of us?"

Grayson shrugged, leaning against the counter with a grin that made his blue eyes crinkle at the corners. "Not much to tell, really. Evie and I had a nice time, that's all. But I'm hoping it won't be the last time we spend together."

His customer gave him a knowing look, but there was a note of genuine warmth in his voice as he clapped Grayson on the shoulder. "Well, good for you, son. She's a fine woman, that Evie. You take care of her, you hear?"

Grayson nodded, feeling a swell of pride and determination rise in his chest. "I will. I promise."

And as the day wound down, with the last of his customers trickling out and the shadows lengthening across the shop floor, Grayson found himself looking forward to the evening ahead, an evening he'd spend with Evie, sharing a meal and talking about all the little things that had begun to matter so much to both of them.

Because even though they were still finding their way, he knew that whatever the future held, they were in it together. And that was more than enough to keep the smile on his face, no matter how many questions Magnolia Springs might throw their way.

Chapter 18

The late autumn sun hung low in the sky over Magnolia Springs, casting long shadows across the town square as the day faded into evening. The chill outside did little to deter the warm, buzzing energy inside Miss Pearl's cozy living room, where the Match Making Club had gathered for another of their highly secretive meetings.

The fire crackled merrily in the hearth, casting a warm glow over the room, where Miss Pearl's friends, Betty, Ruby, and Hattie, sat in their usual spots, cups of hot cocoa or tea in hand. Miss Pearl herself stood near the window, glancing out at the twilight settling over the town, her eyes sharp with the kind of determination that had earned her the unofficial title of Magnolia Springs' matchmaking queen.

"Well, ladies," she began, turning to face the group with a smile that hinted at mischief, "it's been a almost four months since we got Evie and Grayson together, and from what I've seen, they're happy as can be. But I think it's high time we give them a final little nudge toward the next step, don't you agree?"

Betty, perched in the armchair near the window, adjusted her glasses and gave Miss Pearl a knowing look. "Oh, Pearl, you know you've been itching to take things further ever since they started holding hands in public. But I think you're right. Those two are as sweet as sugar together, but if we leave it up to them, they'll be tiptoeing around each other until the cows come home."

Ruby chuckled, setting her tea cup down on the side table with a clink. "I heard that Grayson's been spending more time fixing up that old apartment above his hardware store. If you ask me, he's already thinking about the future, even if he hasn't said it out loud yet."

Hattie, who'd been listening quietly from her spot near the fire, leaned forward with a thoughtful expression. "You know, Pearl, it might not take much to push him in the right direction. A little encouragement, maybe a suggestion that the town wouldn't mind seeing a nice, big wedding in the spring?"

Miss Pearl's smile widened as she clasped her hands together, her eyes gleaming with excitement. "Oh, I think we can do better than that, Hattie. I've got a plan, and it's foolproof."

Betty raised an eyebrow, clearly intrigued. "Foolproof, you say? That's a big claim, Pearl. What exactly do you have in mind?"

Miss Pearl turned, gesturing toward the small table by the window, where a box wrapped in brown paper sat waiting. She picked it up with care, holding it out so the other ladies could see, her smile turning almost conspiratorial.

"It just so happens that my niece is getting married up in Charleston next month," she explained, a hint of pride in her voice. "And I've been talking to Evie about how lovely a winter wedding can be, even in a small town like ours. She's been asking me all kinds of questions, about venues, about dresses, and I could see that little spark in her eyes when she talked about it."

Ruby's eyebrows shot up, and she leaned forward eagerly. "You don't mean—"

Miss Pearl nodded, her smile widening. "Oh, yes, I do. I suggested that maybe Grayson could use a little help with fixing up that apartment of his, just as a way to get them thinking about the future. And I may have hinted that the two of them should come up to Charleston with me for the wedding, just to see how beautiful it can be."

Hattie's eyes widened with understanding, and she clapped her hands together in delight. "A trip to Charleston, just the two of them...

and a wedding to get their hearts stirring! Oh, Pearl, you're a genius! That's bound to get them thinking about taking the plunge themselves."

Betty let out a laugh, shaking her head in admiration. "You're playing the long game, Pearl. Get them all cozy with the idea of a wedding, and then drop a few hints about how nice it would be if Magnolia Springs had a wedding of its own."

Miss Pearl's smile turned sly as she set the box down on the table, her fingers tapping against the paper. "That's not even the best part. Inside this box is an antique engagement ring that belonged to my mother. I've been keeping it for just the right moment, and I think Grayson might appreciate having a little help finding something special for Evie."

Ruby let out a gasp, her hands flying to her mouth. "Oh, Pearl, that's perfect! But how are you going to get him to use it?"

Miss Pearl winked, looking as pleased as a cat with a saucer of cream. "Well, I've already invited Grayson over to the shop next week to help me with a few repairs. I'll just leave the ring where he's sure to find it, along with a little note about how much Evie means to me, and how I'd love for her to have something that's been a part of our Magnolia Springs history. If I know Grayson, he'll take the hint."

Hattie let out a low whistle, shaking her head with a grin. "You really have thought of everything, haven't you? And you're sure he won't feel pressured?"

Miss Pearl's expression softened, and she took a moment to gaze out the window, watching the last of the light fade from the sky. "I know Grayson well enough to see that he's already halfway there, Hattie. He's just been waiting for the right moment, for a sign that it's time to take the next step. And Evie... well, she's never been one to rush into things. But if they both see what could be waiting for them, I think they'll realize they don't have to be afraid."

Ruby nodded, her smile turning gentle. "You're right, Pearl. They've come so far already, and I think they just need a little nudge to see that they're ready for the next chapter. And if that nudge happens to be in the form of a romantic weekend in Charleston and an antique ring, well, who could blame them?"

Betty raised her teacup in a toast, a proud smile on her lips. "To love, ladies, and to a plan that just might be your best one yet, Pearl. Here's hoping we'll be planning a Magnolia Springs wedding before spring comes around."

The women clinked their cups together, their laughter mingling with the crackle of the fire as they settled back into their seats, eager to see their plan unfold. They knew that love wasn't always easy, and that sometimes even the most well-matched hearts needed a little help finding their way. But with Evie and Grayson, they had no doubt that the wait would be worth it.

As the meeting came to a close, Miss Pearl couldn't help but feel a thrill of anticipation for the weeks to come. She imagined the look on Grayson's face when he found the ring, the way his smile would brighten when he realized what it meant. And she pictured Evie's eyes lighting up with joy as she realized that the future she'd dared to dream about was finally within reach.

Because in Magnolia Springs, love had a way of finding its way through even the most unexpected twists and turns, and Miss Pearl intended to make sure that Evie and Grayson's journey reached the happiest ending possible.

The fire continued to crackle, filling the room with a cozy warmth as Miss Pearl and her friends savored their success. Ruby leaned back in her chair, a thoughtful expression crossing her face. "You know, Pearl, if this plan goes off without a hitch, we might need to start working on our next Match making Club's new project."

Hattie leaned forward, her eyes sparkling with mischief. "Well, now that you mention it, I've noticed that Sadie and Wyatt seem to have been spending a little more time together lately. Don't think I haven't seen those shy glances they keep trading at church on Sundays. They definitely need an encouraging shove."

Miss Pearl's smile turned knowing, and she nodded slowly, already considering the possibilities. "Oh, I've got a few ideas for those two, believe me. But first, let's see how things go with our current project. Once we've got a ring on Evie's finger, we'll turn our attention to Sadie and Wyatt."

Betty's laughter filled the room, bright and full of joy. "Oh, Pearl, you're like a dog with a bone when it comes to matchmaking. But I suppose that's why we love you. You've got a heart as big as Magnolia Springs itself, even if you do like to meddle a little too much."

Miss Pearl let out a good-natured laugh, waving away the compliment. "Well, somebody's got to keep this town on its toes. Besides, it's nice to know I'm doing a little good while I'm at it."

With that, the ladies settled into a comfortable silence, each of them imagining the happiness that might soon unfold for Evie and Grayson. Outside, the first snowflakes of the season began to drift down from the darkening sky, turning the town into a quiet, white wonderland.

Miss Pearl glanced out the window, watching the cool winter breeze blow the magnolia tree limbs sway. The same magnolia tree that had seen so many seasons of love come and go. She couldn't help but feel a swell of pride at the thought of helping yet another couple find their way to each other. And as she looked back at her friends, she knew that whatever challenges lay ahead, they would face them together, just as they always had.

The fire crackled one last time, casting a warm glow over the room as the Match Making Club members gathered their things and prepared to head home, their hearts lighter and their minds already planning the next steps.

Meanwhile, Grayson was finishing up his day at the hardware store, his thoughts drifting back to the conversation he'd had with Miss Pearl earlier that morning. She'd mentioned the trip to Charleston, of course, but it was the look in her eyes as she talked about Evie, about how happy she was to see Evie smiling, that had stayed with him.

He'd seen that look before, in the eyes of people who knew what love could mean, who understood how important it was to cherish the people who made life brighter. And as Grayson locked up the shop for the evening, he found himself wondering if maybe Miss Pearl was right, if maybe it was time to take the next step, to make the promises he felt in his heart into something real and lasting.

He glanced at his reflection in the shop's glass door, seeing the uncertainty in his own eyes and wondering how he'd find the right moment to ask Evie to take that step with him. But then he thought about the smile on her face that morning, the way she'd kissed him goodbye with a softness that made his chest ache, and he felt a new sense of determination settle in his bones.

He didn't know exactly how he was going to do it yet, but he knew one thing for certain: he was ready to build a future with Evie, whatever that might look like. And if it took a little courage and a little help from Miss Pearl's not-so-subtle hints, well, he was more than willing to take the leap.

As the days passed, Miss Pearl's plan slowly began to take shape. She made sure to drop by Iris & Ivy whenever she had the chance, chatting with Evie about wedding plans and the beauty of winter ceremonies, planting the seeds of an idea that Evie seemed reluctant to fully consider.

"Now, you've got to admit, a winter wedding has a charm all its own," Miss Pearl said one afternoon, helping Evie arrange a display of poinsettias in the shop window. "There's something about a white dress against freshly fallen snow, don't you think?"

Evie chuckled, shaking her head as she adjusted a ribbon on a bouquet. "Miss Pearl, I think you're getting ahead of yourself. Grayson and I are taking things one day at a time."

Miss Pearl waved a hand, dismissing Evie's caution with a knowing smile. "Oh, pish-posh, Evie. There's nothing wrong with dreaming a little about what the future might hold. And besides, who's to say Grayson isn't thinking about the same things? I hear he's been working on that apartment of his with quite a bit of enthusiasm lately."

Evie paused, a thoughtful expression crossing her face as she considered Miss Pearl's words. "He has been spending a lot of time on the renovations," she admitted, a small, hopeful smile tugging at the corners of her mouth. "I thought maybe he was just looking for a project to keep him busy, but… do you really think he's thinking about us? About a future together?"

Miss Pearl's heart warmed at the uncertainty in Evie's voice, and she reached out to give her a reassuring pat on the arm. "I think Grayson is a man who knows what he wants, Evie. And I think he's got a lot of reasons to want to build something real and lasting with you."

Evie's cheeks flushed with color, but she didn't look away, her fingers fiddling with the ribbon in her hands as she absorbed Miss Pearl's words. "Maybe you're right," she said softly, a new kind of light shining in her eyes. "I guess… I guess I wouldn't mind seeing where that might lead."

Miss Pearl hid her triumphant smile behind a sip of her tea, knowing that the seeds she'd planted were starting to take root. And as she left Iris & Ivy that afternoon, she felt a sense of anticipation building in her chest, knowing that the final piece of her plan was about to fall into place.

A few days later, Grayson found himself at Miss Pearl's tea shop, helping her fix a leaky faucet in the back room. He worked quickly, grateful for the distraction, but as he finished up and wiped his hands on a towel, he noticed a small, neatly wrapped box sitting on the counter.

Miss Pearl caught his curious glance and smiled as she picked up the box, holding it out to him. "I thought you might like to take a look at this, Grayson. It's something that's been in my family for a long time, and I've been thinking about passing it on to someone who might appreciate it."

Grayson frowned slightly, but he accepted the box, unwrapping it with careful fingers. Inside, nestled in a velvet-lined case, was an antique engagement ring, a delicate band of gold set with a beautiful diamond that seemed to catch the light in a way that made it sparkle.

He looked up at Miss Pearl, his breath catching in his throat as realization dawned. "Miss Pearl, I... I don't know what to say. Are you, are you sure?"

Miss Pearl's eyes softened, and she reached out to rest a hand on his shoulder, her voice gentle. "I've never been more sure, Grayson. I know how much Evie means to you, and I know how much you mean to her. And I think she deserves a ring that comes with a little history, don't you?"

Grayson swallowed hard, his fingers brushing over the smooth surface of the ring. He could already picture it on Evie's finger, the way her eyes would light up with surprise and joy when he asked her to marry him. And in that moment, he knew that he couldn't let this chance pass him by, that he was ready to take the next step, no matter how nervous it made him.

He closed the box carefully, tucking it into his pocket with a grateful smile. "Thank you, Miss Pearl. I promise, I'll make sure this ring finds its way to the right person."

Miss Pearl's smile widened, and she gave his arm a reassuring squeeze. "Oh, I have no doubt about that, Grayson. Just remember, sometimes the most important words are the ones you speak from the heart."

As Grayson left the shop, the ring safely tucked in his jacket, he felt a sense of purpose settle in his chest. He didn't know exactly how he was going to do it yet, but he knew that he was going to ask Evie to be his future. And as he walked through streets of Magnolia Springs, his mind already turning over plans for a proposal, he couldn't help but think that maybe, just maybe, this winter would bring more than a possible chance of snow to their little town.

Chapter 19

The late fall morning dawned crisp and bright over Magnolia Springs as Evie and Grayson loaded their bags into the back of Grayson's truck, ready for their weekend trip to Charleston. A soft layer of frost covered the town square, turning the bare branches of the magnolia tree into delicate white lace. The sun cast a golden glow over the rooftops, promising a beautiful, if chilly, day ahead.

Evie pulled her coat tighter around her shoulders, watching Grayson as he carefully placed their overnight bags beside Miss Pearl's suitcase, which was wrapped in a cheerful floral print that seemed to match the older woman's personality. Despite the cold, Grayson wore only a sweater over his flannel shirt, his sleeves pushed up as he worked, and Evie couldn't help but admire the easy strength in his movements.

But beneath her smile, a knot of nervous anticipation twisted in Evie's stomach. This trip would be the first time she and Grayson spent more than a few hours together outside of Magnolia Springs, and the thought of sharing a hotel room made her heart race. It wasn't that she doubted their connection; it was more that she felt the weight of the possibilities hanging between them, possibilities that seemed to grow with every passing day.

"Now, don't you two look like a pair of lovebirds ready for an adventure," Miss Pearl called out cheerfully as she bustled down the flower shop steps, her hands tucked into her coat pockets. Her cheeks were pink from the cold, and her smile was as bright as the winter sun. "I do hope you're ready for a weekend full of romance. Charleston's a special place, you know, perfect for falling in love."

Grayson cleared his throat, offering Miss Pearl a half-smile as he closed the truck's tailgate. "We'll see about that, Miss Pearl. I'm just looking forward to a change of scenery, and I know Evie's excited about seeing all those gardens and old houses."

Evie shot him a playful look, her lips curving into a teasing smile. "You know me too well, Grayson. But I'm sure Miss Pearl's right, Charleston does sound pretty romantic."

Miss Pearl patted Grayson's arm, her eyes twinkling with mischief. "Oh, trust me, dear, you'll see soon enough. And just remember, the best memories are the ones you make when you least expect them."

Evie caught the hint of meaning behind Miss Pearl's words and felt her cheeks warm. She turned to Grayson, hoping he hadn't noticed, but found him giving Miss Pearl a look of amusement mingled with something deeper, a hint of nervousness that mirrored her own. He offered his hand to help her into the passenger seat of the truck, his touch lingering just a moment longer than necessary, sending a pleasant shiver through her.

As they settled into their seats, Miss Pearl climbed into the back, chattering happily about the wedding and her plans for showing them the best of Charleston. Grayson started the engine, and the truck rumbled to life, rolling out of Magnolia Springs and onto the highway that would take them toward the coast.

The drive to Charleston took about 8 hours, winding through small towns and rolling hills, with the sun rising higher in the sky as they traveled eastward. Miss Pearl dozed in the backseat, her head lolling against the window, leaving Evie and Grayson to enjoy the quiet of the open road.

Evie watched the passing scenery, feeling the gentle sway of the truck as they rounded a bend. The rhythmic hum of the engine and the sound of Grayson's deep voice as he told her stories from his childhood filled the air, creating a sense of intimacy that made her heart ache in the best possible way.

"And then there was the time I got stuck on the roof of my parents' house trying to rescue a stray cat," Grayson said with a chuckle, his hands resting casually on the steering wheel. "I must have been about ten. My dad had to get the ladder out, and let's just say I wasn't allowed near that cat again for a while."

Evie laughed softly, imagining a younger version of Grayson, all gangly limbs and wild ideas. "I can just picture it. You've always had that protective streak, haven't you? Even when it gets you into trouble."

Grayson shrugged, but there was a smile tugging at his lips, and he glanced over at her, his gaze lingering for a moment before returning to the road. "Maybe. I like looking out for people. And animals, I guess. But what about you, Evie? Did you ever get into any mischief growing up?"

Evie leaned back in her seat, a wistful smile crossing her face as she thought back to her childhood. "Oh, I wasn't too wild, but I had my moments. Aunt Iris always said I had a stubborn streak, like the time I tried to plant an entire garden in her backyard using only a spoon because I couldn't find a shovel. She let me keep at it until I realized I couldn't even get the seeds an inch deep."

Grayson chuckled, the sound warm and rich. "I can see that. You've got a determination about you, Evie. It's one of the things I admire."

Evie felt her heart skip a beat at his words, and she glanced over at him, catching the sincerity in his expression. There was something in the way he looked at her, something that made her wonder if he was thinking about the same things she was, about the life they might build together if they both took the leap.

They fell into a comfortable silence, each lost in their thoughts as the miles passed beneath the truck's tires. And as the scenery shifted, giving way to the coastal marshes and sprawling oak trees draped in Spanish moss, Evie found herself imagining what it might be like to come home to Grayson every day, to share the little moments and the big ones, to build a future that was theirs alone.

They arrived in Charleston just as the afternoon sun began to dip lower in the sky, casting a golden light over the cobblestone streets and historic buildings. The city was a tapestry of pastel-painted houses and elegant gardens, the air filled with the scent of saltwater and blooming camellias.

Miss Pearl led the way to the small inn where they'd be staying, chattering excitedly about all the sights they had to see before the wedding. Evie and Grayson followed her, exchanging amused smiles as they trailed behind, their shoulders brushing occasionally as they walked.

The inn was charming and cozy, with ivy trailing up the brick facade and a welcoming fire burning in the parlor. Something that had frustrated both Grayson and Evie both, was Miss Pearl's insistence that they have separate rooms. Miss Pearl had said... "It just wasn't proper until they were married." Their rooms were right across the hall from each other, and Evie couldn't help but feel a little flutter of nervousness as she stood with Grayson outside her door, holding her overnight bag in her hands.

"Thank you for bringing me here, Grayson," she said softly, looking up at him. "I didn't realize how much I needed a little getaway."

Grayson's smile was gentle, and he reached out to brush a loose strand of hair behind her ear. "I'm glad you came, Evie. I know it's not Magnolia Springs, but... I hope you enjoy the weekend."

Evie's breath caught at the tenderness in his touch, and for a moment, she thought he might lean in and kiss her right there in the hallway. But instead, he squeezed her hand, then stepped back, offering her a shy smile before retreating to his own room.

That evening, they attended the wedding rehearsal, surrounded by the warmth of Miss Pearl's extended family. The setting was beautiful, an old church with stained-glass windows that glowed in the fading light, and a garden filled with twinkling lights and ivy-draped arches.

Evie couldn't help but be swept up in the romance of it all. She watched the bride and groom practice their vows, their hands clasped tightly as they gazed into each other's eyes, and felt a pang of longing that she hadn't expected. She glanced at Grayson, standing beside her in the church pew, and found him watching her with a soft, unreadable expression.

After the rehearsal, they joined the guests for dinner at a nearby restaurant, but Evie couldn't shake the sense that something important lingered between her and Grayson, something unspoken but pressing. And when Grayson suggested a walk through the quiet streets before heading back to the inn, she agreed, hoping that whatever he needed to say, he might finally find the courage to say it.

They walked through the historic district, passing beneath the glow of wrought-iron streetlamps and the shadows of ancient oak trees. The city seemed to breathe with a life of its own, the cobblestones underfoot echoing with the sounds of distant music and the murmur of the sea.

Grayson kept his hands in his pockets, his steps slow and measured as if he were searching for the right words. Evie walked beside him, her breath clouding in the cool air, and for once, she resisted the urge to fill the silence, sensing that he needed this moment.

Finally, they stopped beneath a canopy of wisteria that clung to an old iron gate, the pale blossoms swaying gently in the night breeze.

Grayson turned to her, his expression serious and filled with a kind of vulnerability that made Evie's heart ache.

"Evie, I... I love you and...," he began, his voice low and hesitant. He reached for her hand, his thumb brushing over her knuckles, and for a moment, it felt like the whole world held its breath.

But then, just as he opened his mouth to continue, a gust of wind rustled through the trees, sending a shiver down Evie's spine. She glanced up at the clouds gathering overhead, feeling the first drops of rain splatter against her face.

Grayson followed her gaze, and the spell was broken. He let out a low chuckle, shaking his head as he pulled her closer under the shelter of the wisteria. "You know I love you too, Grayson. Looks like we've got more rain headed our way. We'd better get back to the inn before we get soaked."

Evie laughed softly, but as they turned back toward the warmth of the inn, she couldn't help but wonder what Grayson had been about to say, and why he'd stopped himself. Still, she took comfort in the feel of his hand in hers, and in the way he kept her close as they hurried through the rain-soaked streets.

And as they reached the inn and kissed each other goodnight at her door, Evie found herself hoping that whatever words he had been searching for, they might find their way into the open before their time in Charleston came to an end.

Chapter 20

The day of Miss Pearl's niece's wedding dawned clear and bright, with the winter sun casting a golden glow over Charleston's historic streets. The air was crisp but not biting, and Evie felt a flutter of excitement in her chest as she stepped out of the inn with Grayson by her side, their arms brushing as they walked toward the little church where the ceremony would take place.

The church stood at the end of a cobblestone lane, its whitewashed walls and arched windows glowing softly in the morning light. Inside, the air was filled with the fragrance of roses and jasmine, garlands of greenery draped over the pews and cascading down from the altar. It was the kind of setting that made Evie's breathe catch, and as she took her seat beside Grayson, she found herself thinking of all the stories she'd heard of love found and celebrated in places just like this.

Evie watched as the bride walked down the aisle, her face radiant beneath her veil, her smile bright with the promise of a new life. The groom's eyes shone with unshed tears as he reached out to take her hand, and Evie felt a lump rise in her throat at the tenderness between them. She glanced at Grayson, who sat beside her with his hands folded in his lap, his expression uncharacteristically serious as he took in the scene before them.

There was something in the way Grayson watched the ceremony, something wistful, almost longing that tugged at Evie's heart. She wondered if he was thinking about what it might be like to stand in the groom's place, to say vows that carried the weight of a lifetime. And though she knew better than to let her imagination run wild, she couldn't help but picture herself in the role of the bride, standing across from Grayson as they made promises to each other.

As the officiant pronounced the couple husband and wife, Evie's hands tightened around the program in her lap, her pulse quickening as she realized that, maybe, the idea of a future with Grayson wasn't so far-fetched after all. And as she glanced over at him, she found him already looking at her, a small, almost shy smile tugging at the corners of his mouth.

"Beautiful, isn't it?" Grayson murmured, his voice low enough that only she could hear. "Makes you think about all the things that really matter."

Evie's smile softened, and she nodded, feeling a warmth spread through her chest. "Yeah, it does. It's a reminder, I guess, of what we're all looking for."

Grayson's gaze held hers for a moment longer, something unspoken passing between them, and Evie's heart fluttered with the feeling that they were standing on the edge of something important, something that neither of them was quite ready to name.

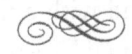

The reception was held in a beautiful courtyard garden behind a historic house, the tables set up beneath twinkling strings of lights and surrounded by camellia bushes that had just begun to bloom. A jazz band played softly in the background as guests mingled, sipping champagne and sharing toasts to the newlyweds.

Evie and Grayson made their way through the crowd, stopping to chat with Miss Pearl and her extended family. Evie found herself caught up in the joy of the celebration, but she couldn't shake the feeling that Grayson was holding something back. He kept glancing around as if searching for something, his hand brushing hers as if he couldn't quite let go.

Every time he seemed on the verge of saying something, they were interrupted, first by Miss Pearl's cousin, who wanted to regale them with a story from her youth, then by a well-meaning uncle who insisted on introducing Grayson to the groom's side of the family. By the time they sat down for dinner, Grayson's shoulders had tensed, and Evie couldn't help but feel a twinge of frustration at the way the evening seemed to be slipping through their fingers.

As they finished their meal, Miss Pearl swooped in with her usual impeccable timing, giving Evie a gentle nudge toward the dessert table. "Now, dear, why don't you go see if there's any of that pecan pie left? I think Grayson and I need a little chat."

Evie glanced between the two of them, sensing that something was afoot, but she nodded and rose from her seat, giving Grayson's arm a reassuring squeeze. "I'll be back in a bit. Don't let Miss Pearl talk your ear off."

Grayson managed a small smile, but as soon as Evie was out of earshot, Miss Pearl's expression turned serious.

"Now, Grayson, I think it's high time you stopped dragging your feet," she said, patting his hand with a firm pat. "That girl of yours is waiting for you to step up, and I'd hate to see you miss your chance."

Grayson swallowed hard, "I know, Miss Pearl. I've been trying, but every time I think I've found the right moment, something comes up. What if she's not ready? What if... what if I mess this up?"

Miss Pearl gave him a knowing look, her smile turning gentle. "Grayson Bennett, you've faced down storms, handled stubborn customers, and helped build a home for yourself here in Magnolia Springs. You think you can't handle a little thing like asking the woman you love to marry you?"

Grayson let out a shaky laugh, rubbing the back of his neck as he looked out over the garden, where Evie was chatting with Miss Pearl's niece by the dessert table. She looked so beautiful in the soft light of the lanterns, her laughter mingling with the music in a way that made his heart ache. "You make it sound so simple, Miss Pearl."

Miss Pearl squeezed his shoulder, her voice turning soft with encouragement. "It's simple if you let it be, dear. Just tell her how you feel. Everything else will fall into place."

Grayson took a deep breath. "Okay. Tonight. I won't let another chance go by."

※

As the reception wound down and the last of the guests began to depart, Grayson finally took Evie's hand, his grip firm and a little shaky. "Hey, I have something I want to show you. Do you mind taking a walk with me?"

Evie blinked in surprise, but the hopeful look in his eyes made her smile. "Of course, Grayson. Lead the way."

He guided her through the courtyard and out onto the quiet streets, the sound of their footsteps echoing softly off the cobblestones. The night air was cool, but Evie hardly noticed as they walked side by side, her hand warm in his. She couldn't help but wonder what had him so nervous, but she didn't press him, sensing that whatever he needed to say, he would find the right moment for it.

They turned down a narrow lane that led to a hidden garden behind a historic inn, the space lit by lanterns that cast a soft, golden glow over the ivy-covered walls. A small fountain burbled quietly in the center of the garden, the water catching the light like scattered jewels. It was a place that seemed made for secrets and confessions, and Evie felt her breath catch as Grayson led her to the edge of the fountain, his expression serious and intent.

"Evie, there's something I need to tell you," he began, his voice low and rough with emotion. He reached into his pocket, his fingers brushing against the velvet box, but the words seemed to stick in his throat, his nerves getting the better of him.

Evie looked up at him, her brows furrowing with concern. "Grayson, you're starting to worry me. Whatever it is, you can tell me."

Grayson swallowed hard, his heart pounding in his chest as he met her gaze. But just as he was about to speak, the sky above them rumbled with the deep roll of thunder, and a sudden burst of rain spilled from the clouds, drenching them both in seconds.

Evie let out a startled laugh, raising her hands to shield herself from the downpour. "Oh my gosh, Grayson, we need to get inside!"

Grayson blinked, the moment slipping away like water through his fingers, but he couldn't help the smile that tugged at his lips as Evie grabbed his hand, pulling him back toward the inn. They ran through the rain, laughing like children, their clothes soaked through and their hair plastered to their faces.

When they reached the shelter of the inn's porch, panting and dripping wet, Grayson turned to her, unable to keep the words back any longer. "Evie, I—"

But Evie cut him off with a kiss, pressing her cold lips to his in a gesture that stole the breath from his lungs. She pulled back, her cheeks flushed and her smile as bright as the lantern light. "Whatever you're going to say, it can wait. Let's just enjoy tonight, okay?"

Grayson's chest ached with the words he hadn't spoken, but he nodded, his fingers brushing a lock of wet hair from her face. "Okay, Evie. But soon. I promise."

And as they stepped inside, leaving the rain behind, Grayson vowed to himself that the next chance he got, he wouldn't let it slip away. Because he knew now, with a certainty that went bone-deep, that Evie was the future he wanted, rainstorms, laughter, and all.

Chapter 21

The return to Magnolia Springs brought with it a familiar comfort for Evie and Grayson. The town square, with its charming shops and twinkling holiday lights, felt like a warm embrace, especially after the whirlwind of their Charleston weekend. As they pulled into the driveway behind Iris & Ivy, Evie couldn't help but let out a contented sigh, glancing at Grayson as he parked the truck.

"Home sweet home," she murmured, smiling as she caught his eye.

Grayson returned her smile, his blue eyes crinkling at the corners in that way that always made her heart skip a beat. "Yeah, it feels good to be back. I missed it, missed *you*, too."

Evie's cheeks flushed at his words, a familiar warmth spreading through her chest. But as they gathered their bags from the back of the truck, she couldn't quite shake the sense that something was still hanging between them, something unspoken. She had caught glimpses of Grayson's hesitance during their trip, moments when he seemed ready to share something important but then pulled back, as if waiting for the perfect time.

She told herself not to worry, that Grayson would share whatever was on his mind when he was ready. But as they walked up the back steps to the flower shop, she found herself glancing at him, wondering if that moment might come sooner rather than later.

The next day, while Evie busied herself at Iris & Ivy, Grayson found himself standing outside Miss Pearl's shop, the cold wind biting at his cheeks. He took a deep breath, steadying his nerves before stepping inside, where he was immediately greeted by the cozy warmth of the wood stove and the scent of freshly baked gingerbread.

Miss Pearl was behind the counter, rearranging a display of handmade ornaments, and she looked up with a smile as Grayson entered. "Well, well, if it isn't our favorite hardware man. What can I do for you today, Grayson? More advice on matters of the heart?"

Grayson rubbed the back of his neck, feeling a little sheepish but determined. "Actually, Miss Pearl, I could use your help, yours and the ladies', if they're up for it. I... I want to propose to Evie, and I want it to be perfect. Something that feels like home to both of us."

Miss Pearl's eyes lit up, and she clapped her hands together, her smile spreading wide. "Oh, Grayson, that's wonderful! I knew you had it in you. Now, tell me what you have in mind, and we'll make sure it's a moment Evie will never forget."

Grayson took a deep breath, glancing around the shop as if gathering his thoughts. "Well, I was thinking about the town park, how beautiful it looks in the winter. I thought maybe we could set it up with lights, make it look like a winter wonderland. Somewhere special, where she'll feel like... like this town really is where she belongs."

Miss Pearl's smile softened, and she reached out to squeeze his arm, her voice warm with approval. "Oh, Grayson, that's a lovely idea. Evie will adore it. And don't you worry, we'll take care of all the details. I'll get Ruby, Betty, and Hattie on board, and we'll have that park shining like the North Star."

Grayson's shoulders relaxed with relief, and he managed a grateful smile. "Thank you, Miss Pearl. I know I've been dragging my feet, but I want this to be right. I want her to know how much I love her."

Miss Pearl patted his arm, her eyes twinkling with pride. "She already knows, dear. But this will show her, loud and clear. Now, you leave the decorations to us, and you focus on making sure Evie is right where she needs to be when the time comes."

Grayson nodded, feeling a renewed sense of determination settle in his chest. As he left Miss Pearl's shop, he couldn't help but imagine the look on Evie's face when she saw what they'd planned for her, the surprise, the joy, and, hopefully, the answer he was waiting for.

The next few days were a blur of quiet planning and secret preparations. While Evie spent her time tending to the flower shop, Miss Pearl, Ruby, Betty, and Hattie busied themselves at the park, stringing twinkling lights between the oak trees and draping evergreen garlands over the benches and gazebo.

A surprise snowfall arrived just in time, coating the park in a blanket of pristine white that sparkled beneath the lights. It looked like a scene from a storybook, and as the last decorations were put in place, Miss Pearl couldn't help but feel a thrill of satisfaction at how beautiful it had turned out.

"Now, don't forget, Grayson, you'll need to keep Evie occupied until sunset," she reminded him as she inspected the final touches. "We'll be here, making sure everything's perfect for when you two arrive."

Grayson nodded, glancing around the transformed park with a mix of gratitude and awe. "I don't know how to thank you all. It's more than I could have hoped for."

Hattie waved a hand, her cheeks pink with the cold. "Oh, hush now, Grayson. This is what we live for, bringing a little romance to this town. Just make sure you get down on one knee when the time's right, and don't let those nerves get the best of you."

Grayson chuckled softly, tucking his hands into his pockets to ward off the chill. "I'll try my best. And... I really appreciate this, all of you. I just hope she says yes."

Ruby gave him a reassuring pat on the back. "Oh, she will, dear. Anyone with eyes can see how much she cares for you. Now go on, get ready for your big moment."

※

That evening, as the sun began to set, Grayson arrived at Iris & Ivy to find Evie locking up the shop, a hint of curiosity in her expression as she spotted him waiting by the door. She raised an eyebrow, glancing at his outstretched hand. "What's this? A surprise visit?"

Grayson smiled, offering his hand to her. "I was hoping you'd join me for a walk. There's something I want to show you."

Evie hesitated for a moment, a playful smile tugging at her lips. "You're being mysterious again, Grayson Bennett. But I'll play along, lead the way."

She slipped her hand into his, and they set off through the town square, the cold air nipping at their cheeks. The snow crunched softly beneath their boots, and Evie felt a shiver run through her, not from the cold, but from the warmth of Grayson's hand wrapped around hers.

As they neared the town park, she noticed the glow of lights spilling through the trees, casting a soft, magical light over the snow-covered path. She glanced up at Grayson, her brow furrowing in confusion. "What's going on here?"

Grayson's smile was gentle, but there was a nervous energy behind it that made her heart race. "You'll see, Evie. Just a little further."

They rounded the bend, and Evie stopped in her tracks, her breath catching in her throat as she took in the sight before her. The park was transformed, twinkling lights draped from the branches and casting a warm glow over the snow. The gazebo was wrapped in garlands, and lanterns lined the path, flickering gently in the evening breeze.

"Grayson, this is... it's beautiful," Evie whispered, turning to look at him with wide, astonished eyes. "Did you, did you do all of this?"

Grayson nodded, his expression turning serious as he took both of her hands in his. "I had a little help from Miss Pearl and her friends. But I wanted to give you something special, something that feels like home."

Evie's heart swelled at his words, and she felt a lump rise in her throat as she looked around the enchanted scene. "Grayson, I don't know what to say..."

Grayson squeezed her hands, drawing her closer until their breath mingled in the cold night air. "You don't have to say anything, Evie. Just... come with me."

He led her toward the gazebo, where the lanterns cast soft shadows over the snow. And as they stood beneath the twinkling lights, surrounded by the beauty of the night, Grayson took a deep breath, gathering his courage for the words he'd held back for too long.

Evie looked up at him, her eyes shining with emotion, and she had a feeling that whatever was about to happen, it would change everything between them.

Grayson led Evie up the steps of the gazebo, their steps crunching softly on the fresh snow. The twinkling lights reflected in Evie's wide eyes as she looked around, taking in every detail of the scene that had been lovingly crafted just for her. She turned to Grayson, her cheeks pink from the cold, but her expression was one of pure wonder.

"Grayson, this is... it's like something out of a dream," she whispered, her voice trembling with emotion. "I don't know what I did to deserve all of this."

Grayson swallowed hard, feeling his heart thud against his ribs as he held her hands tighter, willing himself to keep his voice steady. "You deserve all of this and more, Evie. You've brought so much light into my life... more than I ever thought I'd find again."

Evie's breath caught at the sincerity in his words, her eyes searching his face as if trying to read the thoughts that flickered behind his blue gaze. "Grayson, what's this all about? Is there... something you're trying to tell me?"

He took a deep breath, letting the cool night air fill his lungs, and then he slowly lowered himself to one knee, reaching into his pocket to pull out the small black velvet box. Evie's eyes widened, her hands flying to her mouth as a gasp escaped her.

"Evie," Grayson began, his voice raw with emotion as he looked up at her, "I know I've taken my time getting to this point, but it's only because I wanted to get it right. I wanted to make sure that when I asked you to spend the rest of your life with me, you'd know that it came from the deepest part of my heart."

He opened the box, revealing the antique ring that had once belonged to Miss Pearl's mother, the diamond catching the light in a way that made it shine like a star against the backdrop of snow. Evie's eyes filled with tears, her hands trembling as she reached out to touch the ring with gentle fingers.

"Evie Matthews, you're the best thing that's ever happened to me, and I don't want to spend another day without knowing that you'll be by my side. Will you marry me?"

For a moment, the world seemed to hold its breath, the snow falling softly around them as the night grew still. Evie's vision blurred with tears, and she blinked rapidly, trying to focus on the man kneeling before her, the man who had turned her life upside down in the most beautiful way.

She dropped to her knees in front of him, her hands cupping his face as she nodded, her smile so bright it lit up the night. "Yes, Grayson. Yes, I'll marry you."

Grayson let out a laugh that was half a sob, his own eyes growing misty as he slipped the ring onto her finger, the band fitting perfectly as if it had been made for her all along. And then he pulled her into his arms, holding her tight as they knelt together in the snow, their laughter and tears mingling with the joy that seemed to fill the world around them.

They kissed beneath the glowing lights of the gazebo, the cold forgotten in the warmth of each other's embrace. Evie clung to Grayson as if she never wanted to let go, her heart bursting with a happiness she had never thought possible. And as she looked down at the ring that sparkled on her finger, she knew that this, this moment, this man, was everything she had been waiting for.

Grayson held her close, his forehead resting against hers as he whispered, "I promise, Evie, I'm going to spend the rest of my life making you as happy as you've made me tonight."

Evie's breath hitched, and she pressed her lips to his in a kiss that tasted of hope and new beginnings. "You already have, Grayson. You already have."

Later that night, Evie and Grayson walked back to her flower shop, their hands entwined and their hearts full. The snow fell softly around them, muffling the sounds of the town, and the lights in the shop windows cast a golden glow over the snowy ground.

They paused on the front steps, and Grayson pulled Evie into his arms, his gaze filled with a love that made her breath catch. "I meant what I said, Evie. You're my home now. And I promise I'll never stop trying to make you smile."

Evie reached up, cupping his face with her hands as she kissed him softly, her heart swelling with a love that she knew would only grow stronger with time. "And I promise to love you, Grayson Bennett, through every season, through every snowfall, and through every moment that lies ahead."

Grayson's arms tightened around her, holding her close as they stood together in the quiet of the night, the snow swirling around them like a blessing. And as they kissed beneath the twinkling lights of the town they both cherished, they knew that whatever challenges might come their way, they would face them together, hand in hand, heart to heart, forever.

Chapter 22

Evie leaned heavily against the counter of Iris & Ivy, clutching her oversized mug of coffee like a lifeline. She blinked blearily at the front window, where the morning sun was just beginning to spill into the shop, casting warm rays over the carefully arranged flower displays. Despite the exhaustion that tugged at her, courtesy of a long night of *celebrating* with Grayson, the smile on her face was impossible to erase.

Every time she closed her eyes, she could still see the twinkling lights of the park, the snow falling gently around them, and Grayson's face as he slipped that beautiful antique ring onto her finger. She glanced down at her hand now, turning it this way and that to admire the way the diamond caught the light. It felt almost surreal, like a dream she hadn't quite woken up from.

Just as she took another sip of her coffee, the front door burst open with the force of a small hurricane, as Clara and Sadie came skidding into the shop. Clara was practically vibrating with excitement, her curls bouncing with every step, while Sadie, usually more composed and shy, was talking a mile a minute, her cheeks flushed with the cold.

"Oh my gosh, Evie, we *heard* the news! Tell us everything!" Clara practically shouted, her voice echoing through the quiet shop as she grabbed Evie's hands and tugged her closer to the counter.

"Everything!" Sadie echoed, waving her arms for emphasis. "You can't leave out a single detail! How did he do it? Did he get down on one knee? Was it romantic? Was there music playing? Did you cry? Oh, I bet you cried. I would have cried!"

Evie barely had a chance to take a breath before Clara chimed in again, her words tripping over themselves in her eagerness. "And let me see the ring! Oh, wow, it's even prettier than Miss Pearl said! And when's the wedding? Are you going to have it here in Magnolia Springs? You have to! The whole town is buzzing about it!"

Evie laughed, holding up her hands as if to fend off the barrage of questions. "Okay, okay, slow down, you two! I'll tell you everything, but one at a time, please! I haven't even finished my first cup of coffee."

Clara and Sadie exchanged a glance, then both grabbed chairs and dragged them up to the counter, settling in like they were preparing for a juicy story. Clara leaned forward, her chin resting in her hands, while Sadie fanned herself with a magazine she'd swiped from the front display.

"All right, spill it, Evie!" Clara urged, her eyes sparkling. "We want every romantic, sappy detail. Did he give a big speech about how he's loved you from the moment he met you?"

Evie shook her head, still grinning as she tried to piece together the whirlwind of the night before. "It wasn't a big speech, Clara. But he did take me to the park, and it was all lit up with those beautiful twinkling lights... and then he got down on one knee, and it just felt so... right, you know? And no, we don't want to wait months for a wedding, we want it as soon as possible."

Sadie clutched her chest dramatically, her eyes welling with tears. "Oh, I knew it! I *knew* he was going to propose after that trip to Charleston. I told Clara, didn't I, Clara? I said, 'Mark my words, that man is going to put a ring on her finger before the first snowfall,' and look, I was *right*!"

Clara rolled her eyes playfully. "Yeah, yeah, Sadie, we all know you're the town psychic now. But come on, Evie, tell us the real juicy stuff! Like, what was the first thing he said after you said yes? Was he all teary-eyed too?"

Evie laughed, her cheeks flushing as she remembered the way Grayson had looked at her, his eyes shining with emotion. "Honestly, we were both laughing and crying at the same time. It wasn't perfect, it was messy and wonderful and... just so *us*. And yes, he was a little teary, but don't you dare tell him I told you that!"

Clara clapped her hands together, her grin widening. "Oh, Evie, this is *exactly* what I needed to hear this morning. I swear, the whole town is talking about nothing else. And you should hear some of the rumors flying around! Someone told me they heard that Grayson rode up on horseback, like some kind of knight in shining armor."

Sadie snorted, shaking her head. "That's nothing! I heard that there was a runaway carriage involved, and Grayson had to chase it down before he could pop the question! Can you imagine?"

Evie buried her face in her hands, laughing so hard she nearly spilled her coffee. "Oh my goodness, you're kidding, right? Where do people come up with this stuff?"

Clara winked, nudging her playfully. "Hey, you know how it is in Magnolia Springs. Give them an inch, and they'll weave a whole fairy tale out of it. And honestly, we're just glad to have something to gossip about. The only excitement we've had lately was Ruby's cat getting stuck on top of the water tower, and that got old fast."

Sadie leaned closer, her voice dropping to a conspiratorial whisper. "Oh, and Miss Pearl's been strutting around town like a peacock, telling everyone how she 'knew all along' that you two were meant to be. I'm pretty sure she's already planning your wedding, even though she hasn't mentioned it to you yet."

Evie rolled her eyes fondly, though she couldn't help but smile. "That sounds like Miss Pearl. She's been behind this whole thing from the start, hasn't she? I can't believe she's already planning a wedding. I haven't even had time to think about what kind of wedding we want yet! We just want it soon."

Clara patted her hand, her expression turning sympathetic. "Oh, don't worry, Evie. You know Miss Pearl, she'll have half the town signed up to help with the wedding before you can even blink. And honestly, it'll probably be the event of the season."

Just as they were all laughing over the thought of Miss Pearl organizing the town's social calendar, the bell over the shop door jangled again, and who should waltz in but Miss Pearl herself, wearing a satisfied smile and carrying a basket of muffins.

"Good morning, ladies! I hope I'm not interrupting anything too serious," she said, setting the basket down on the counter and helping herself to a seat. "I couldn't be happier for you and Grayson."

Evie smiled, feeling her heart warm at Miss Pearl's genuine enthusiasm. "Thank you, Miss Pearl. I'm still getting used to the idea myself."

Miss Pearl waved a hand dismissively, her eyes twinkling. "Oh, nonsense! You'll have plenty of time to get used to it while we plan the most beautiful wedding Magnolia Springs has ever seen. Now, I was thinking we should start with a nice little engagement party, something cozy, with just a few friends."

Clara snickered, leaning over to whisper in Evie's ear. "Translation: She's inviting half the town."

Evie stifled a laugh, nodding at Miss Pearl as she tried to keep a straight face. "That sounds lovely, Miss Pearl. But, really, we don't want an engagement party or anything too large or too fancy we just want the wedding..."

Miss Pearl patted Evie's hand, her smile as sweet as the muffins she'd brought. "Oh, don't you worry, dear. We'll keep it *just* small enough to be intimate but big enough that everyone will have a chance to wish you well. And I've already got a few ideas for the theme! Maybe something with a winter wonderland feel, to match that beautiful proposal in the snow!"

Sadie leaned in, her eyes wide with excitement. "Oh, I love that! We could use white roses and twinkle lights, ooh, and maybe have hot cocoa for everyone! It'll be so romantic!"

Evie rolled her eyes as head spun with all the suggestions, but she couldn't help but feel a warm glow of gratitude for the people around her. As chaotic as they could be, Clara, Sadie, and Miss Pearl were part of the heart of Magnolia Springs, the part that had made this town feel like home. "We want it soon, Miss Pearl and the snow from yesterday has already melted. It's Georgia and I not waiting another five years for another snowfall to get married."

And as she looked down at the ring on her finger, she couldn't help but feel that, with their support and Grayson by her side, whatever the future held, it was sure to be filled with laughter, love, and just a little bit of gossip.

Clara giggles as she leaned back in her chair, balancing it on two legs as she reached for a muffin from Miss Pearl's basket, her expression turning mischievous. "You know, Evie, there's also a rumor going around that Grayson's planning to whisk you away to some tropical island for the honeymoon. What do you think of that? Maybe a little sand, sun, and... oh, I don't know, more of that celebrating you were up to last night?"

Evie nearly choked on her coffee, sputtering as she set her mug down quickly. "Clara! You know that's not true! We barely know where we're going to have the wedding, let alone the honeymoon!"

Clara shrugged, a playful grin spreading across her face as she nudged Sadie with her elbow. "Hey, I'm just repeating what I heard down at the diner this morning. You know, our dear Grayson has quite the reputation now, half the ladies at the café were talking about how he's the town's most romantic man."

Sadie nodded eagerly, her eyes wide with mock seriousness. "Oh, absolutely. I heard he's even planning to ride a white horse down Main

Street on your wedding day. Someone said they saw him talking to Frank over at the stables about it."

Evie's laughter bubbled up, uncontrollable and bright. She pressed a hand to her chest, trying to catch her breath. "Oh, please! Grayson is not planning anything like that."

Miss Pearl chimed in, a sly smile playing at the corners of her mouth. "Well, dear, you never know. Love makes people do some wild things."

Clara and Sadie gasped, their expressions turning hopeful. "Evie! Maybe Grayson will sing to you! Can you imagine him strumming a guitar on the front steps of Iris & Ivy?"

Evie snorted, covering her face with her hands. "Okay, now you're all just being ridiculous. Grayson is many things, but a guitar-playing troubadour is not one of them. I'm pretty sure he'd rather wrestle a grizzly bear than sing in public."

Miss Pearl gave her a wink, her eyes twinkling with amusement. "Well, dear, stranger things have happened in this town, haven't they?"

Before Evie could respond, the bell over the shop door jingled again, and another familiar face poked inside, this time, it was Ruby, holding a tray of freshly baked scones wrapped in a gingham cloth. "Am I too late for the gossip?"

Clara immediately waved her over. "Not at all, Ruby! Pull up a chair! We were just getting to the good part, did you hear about the runaway carriage during the proposal?"

Ruby's eyes widened, and she set the tray down on the counter before taking a seat, her expression eager. "Oh, I heard something about that, but I didn't get all the details. Was there really a carriage? And was Grayson actually wearing a tuxedo? Someone told me they saw him in tails!"

Evie groaned, shaking her head with a laugh as she buried her face in her hands. "Oh, for the love of magnolias! No, Ruby, there was no carriage, no tuxedo, and definitely no tails. It was just the two of us in the park with some lights and snow."

Ruby pouted, clearly disappointed by the lack of theatrics. "Well, that's no fun! But I guess it's sweet in its own way. And, you know, that ring really does look beautiful, Evie. It suits you."

Evie's smile softened, and she glanced down at the antique ring that sparkled on her finger, feeling a fresh wave of warmth wash over her. "Thanks, Ruby. It really is special. Grayson said it's an heirloom from Miss Pearl's family. I can't believe he thought to ask her for something so meaningful."

Miss Pearl beamed, her chest swelling with pride. "I was never blessed with children to hand the ring down to. Grayson knows a good thing when he sees it. And he knew that ring would be perfect for you, Evie. It's got a history, just like this town, and now you'll be a part of it too."

Sadie wiped an imaginary tear from her eye, her voice turning theatrical. "Oh, it's just so beautiful! I'm going to need tissues if this keeps up. And speaking of beautiful, Evie, you'd better believe I'm helping plan this wedding. I've already got a Pinterest board full of ideas!"

Clara shot her a look of mock indignation. "Sadie, please. *I* was going to help with the planning first. We're going to need a whole committee to make this wedding as perfect as it deserves to be!"

Miss Pearl raised a hand, cutting in before they could argue further. "Now, now, girls, there's plenty of work to go around, and I'm sure Evie will appreciate all the help she can get. Besides, I've already started making a list of everything we'll need for the engagement party."

Evie couldn't help but laugh at the sheer enthusiasm radiating from the small crowd gathered in her shop. It was chaotic, it was overwhelming, but it was also one of the most heartwarming mornings she could remember. As much as she teased Miss Pearl, Clara, and

Sadie, she knew she wouldn't trade their support for anything in the world.

She reached out, giving Miss Pearl's hand a squeeze. "Thank you, all of you. Really. I'm so lucky to have such wonderful friends, and honestly, I wouldn't have it any other way."

Miss Pearl patted her hand, her smile softening with affection. "We're the lucky ones, Evie. It's not every day you get to watch two people find their way to each other like you and Grayson have. And don't you worry, your wedding is going to be just as special as your engagement, even if we have to drag that man onto a white horse ourselves."

Evie rolled her eyes good-naturedly, a laugh bubbling up again. "Let's just stick to keeping Grayson on the ground, okay? But really, thank you, Miss Pearl. You've done so much for us, and I don't know how I'll ever repay you."

Miss Pearl shook her head, her expression turning serious for a moment. "Just be happy, Evie. That's all the thanks I'll ever need."

As the morning wore on, the gossip gradually turned to other matters, Ruby's scone recipe, and Sadie's latest attempt at online dating, and Clara's ongoing quest to find the perfect Christmas tree for her apartment. But through it all, Evie couldn't stop smiling, feeling the joy of her friends and the love of her new fiancé wrap around her like a warm blanket.

When the last of the scones had been eaten and Miss Pearl and the others had finally taken their leave, promising to return soon with more plans, Evie sat down at the counter and let out a long, contented sigh. She wrapped her hands around her now-cold coffee, gazing out at the snow-covered town square, and felt a deep sense of peace settle in her heart.

She thought back to the early days when she'd first moved to Magnolia Springs, how uncertain she'd felt, how unsure she was of where she fit into this close-knit community. Now, looking down at the ring on her finger and thinking of the people who had become her family, she couldn't imagine being anywhere else.

Evie knew that the next few weeks would be filled with planning and preparation, with ups and downs and a lot more unsolicited advice from Miss Pearl. But she also knew that, with Grayson by her side and her friends cheering them on, they would navigate it all together, one laugh, one cup of coffee, and one heartfelt moment at a time.

And for the first time in her life, she truly believed that her own little corner of Magnolia Springs might just be the start of the happiest chapter yet.

Chapter 23

Miss Pearl's cozy living room buzzed with excitement as the ladies of Magnolia Springs' unofficial Match Making Club gathered for their latest meeting. The smell of cinnamon and freshly brewed tea filled the air, mingling with the crackle of the fireplace, where a merry flame danced. The ladies were in high spirits, ready to tackle their next project: Evie and Grayson's upcoming wedding.

Miss Pearl, seated in her favorite floral armchair, clapped her hands to get everyone's attention, though it wasn't easy with Ruby and Betty chattering about the best places to rent tablecloths. She cleared her throat dramatically, her eyes gleaming with mischief as she surveyed her friends.

"All right, ladies, it's time to put our heads together and make sure Evie and Grayson have the wedding of their dreams," she declared, leaning forward with a conspiratorial smile. "We've already helped get them this far, now it's up to us to make sure their special day is one to remember."

Ruby adjusted her glasses, her notepad already filled with scribbled ideas. "I've been thinking, what if we use magnolias for the centerpieces? It would be a lovely touch, don't you think? After all, it's Magnolia Springs, and Evie's shop is called *Iris & Ivy*."

Betty, never one to be outdone, waved her hand dismissively. "Oh, sure, Ruby, that's a nice idea, but what about the food? We can't have a wedding without a proper southern feast. I've got a cousin who makes the best shrimp and grits this side of the Mississippi, and I'm sure he'd be happy to cater, just so long as he can bring his banjo."

Hattie, perched on the edge of the couch, leaned in, her eyes sparkling. "Forget the food for a minute! We need to think about entertainment. I heard Evie likes to dance, but Grayson... well, he's got two left feet if you ask me. We should probably arrange for a little dance lesson for him before he makes a fool of himself on the dance floor."

Miss Pearl shook her head, though she couldn't hide her smile. "Now, now, Hattie, let's not embarrass the poor boy. He's got enough on his mind, what with planning a life with Evie. But I do agree that we need to make sure this wedding is memorable. Ruby, you're in charge of the flowers. Betty, you handle the food, let's make it feel like a real Magnolia Springs celebration. And Hattie, you can work on finding us a band. Something that'll get folks on their feet."

Hattie sat up straighter, already tapping her fingers on her knee as if testing out potential rhythms. "I'll see if that old bluegrass band from the fall festival is available. They'd bring just the right kind of charm."

As the conversation flowed, the women leaned in closer, their voices dropping to a hush as they moved on to the inevitable gossip portion of the meeting. Clara, who had been hovering in the kitchen doorway, finally came in with a tray of cookies, eager to join in on the fun.

"You know, Evie's been glowing like a lantern ever since that proposal," Clara remarked, setting the tray down with a grin. "I ran into her this morning, and she couldn't stop smiling. It's so sweet, but... I also heard that Sadie saw them kissing in front of the flower shop last night, and apparently, it was the kind of kiss that would make a preacher blush!"

Betty gasped, fanning herself with a napkin. "Oh, my stars, Clara, you don't say! And in public, too? Well, I never!"

Hattie chuckled, shaking her head. "Come on, Betty, it's about time those two stopped being so shy. Besides, if I were Evie, I'd be kissing that handsome Grayson every chance I got! Did you see him at the church social last month? That man could charm the stripes off a tiger."

Ruby nodded sagely, leaning closer as if sharing a secret. "Well, I heard from Helen at the bakery that Grayson's been making plans for their honeymoon. She swears he ordered a whole box of travel brochures for Hawaii and the Caribbean. If that doesn't say romance, I don't know what does."

Miss Pearl clucked her tongue, though her eyes gleamed with pride. "Oh, I knew those two would make a good pair, and now look at them, planning a wedding, thinking about a future. It just goes to show that sometimes a little nudge is all it takes."

The group shared a round of knowing smiles, but Miss Pearl's expression turned thoughtful as she glanced toward the window. "Speaking of nudges, ladies, I think we need to discuss our next project." Miss Pearl's smile turned positively devious as she said. "Well, I've been thinking about Sadie and Wyatt as we've discussed. They've been dancing around each other for months now, but they're too shy to make a move. I believe it's high time we give them a little push."

Betty clapped her hands together, barely able to contain her excitement. "Oh, that's a wonderful idea! Sadie's always talking about how there aren't any good men left in town, but we all know she's had her eye on Wyatt since last summer."

Ruby leaned in, her voice dropping to a conspiratorial whisper. "You know, I heard Wyatt's been asking around about where Sadie likes to go for coffee. If that's not a sign, I don't know what is!"

Clara, perched on the edge of her seat, practically bounced with excitement. "Oh, we could arrange for them to bump into each other at the café! Or maybe get them both signed up for the same dance class... just imagine Sadie in Wyatt's arms! It'd be like one of those romance novels she's always reading."

Miss Pearl waved her hand, settling them down before they got too carried away. "Let's not rush into it just yet, but it's good to keep some ideas in our back pocket. First things first, let's focus on Evie and

Grayson's big day. But after that... well, Sadie and Wyatt are definitely next on the list."

Hattie smirked, crossing her arms over her chest. "Poor things don't even know what's coming, do they? I almost feel sorry for them."

Miss Pearl's eyes twinkled with mischief as she looked around the room, her gaze landing on each of her friends in turn. "Oh, Hattie, where's the fun in letting them know? Half the joy of matchmaking is watching them realize what's right in front of their noses."

The ladies erupted into laughter, the kind that made the walls of Miss Pearl's cozy living room shake with warmth. They settled back into their seats, sharing stories and ideas, with Ruby sketching out centerpiece designs, Betty scribbling down recipes, and Hattie humming potential songs for the wedding playlist.

Miss Pearl, ever the orchestrator of romantic chaos, sat back with a satisfied smile, her heart full as she imagined the joy that lay ahead for Evie, Grayson, and whoever else happened to fall into the sights of the Match Making Club. There was something truly special about helping people find love, and Miss Pearl intended to keep doing it for as long as she could.

As the meeting wound down, she raised her teacup in a toast, her voice ringing with pride. "To love, ladies, to making sure it finds its way, even if it needs a little help from time to time."

The others lifted their cups, their faces glowing with the satisfaction of a job well done. "To love!" they echoed, their voices blending with the crackle of the fire.

And with that, the Match Making Club was back in business, ready to tackle wedding plans, meddle in the love lives of their neighbors, and ensure that no heart in Magnolia Springs went unpaired for long.

Chapter 24

Evie and Grayson sat across from each other in the cozy kitchen of Evie's apartment above *Iris & Ivy*, a notebook sprawled open on the table between them. The morning light filtered in through the window, catching the steam rising from their coffee cups. A plate of homemade muffins, courtesy of Miss Pearl, naturally, sat untouched in the middle of the table.

Grayson rubbed the back of his neck, glancing down at the list they'd started. "So, I was thinking we could keep the ceremony small. Just a few close friends and family…"

Evie looked up, a teasing smile tugging at her lips. "Grayson, we both know this is Magnolia Springs. There's no such thing as a small event here. Miss Pearl will insist on inviting half the town, and if we don't, she'll never let us hear the end of it."

Grayson groaned, leaning back in his chair. "You're right. She's probably already sent out invitations without us knowing." He cast her a sidelong glance, his tone turning more serious. "But what do *you* want, Evie? I don't want you to feel overwhelmed by this whole thing."

Evie reached across the table, taking his hand in hers. The touch grounded her, reminding her of how far they'd come. "Honestly, I just want a day that feels like us. I don't care if the whole town is there, as long as I get to marry you at the end of it."

Grayson's expression softened, and he brought her hand to his lips, brushing a kiss across her knuckles. "You've got a deal, then. We'll make sure it's a day that's all about *us*, even if we have to share it with a few dozen of Miss Pearl's closest friends."

Evie laughed, a lightness in her chest as they began to sketch out ideas for the ceremony and reception. But just as they were starting to settle on a vision, a knock sounded at the door, followed almost immediately by the unmistakable voice of Miss Pearl.

Within minutes, Miss Pearl had made herself at home in Evie's kitchen, settling into a chair and pulling out her own notepad. Ruby, Betty, and Hattie weren't far behind, each armed with clipboards, swatches, and enough enthusiasm to organize a state fair.

Grayson shot Evie a look as he refilled the coffee pot, silently mouthing, *Here we go.* Evie stifled a laugh and braced herself for what was sure to be a whirlwind of suggestions.

"I've been thinking about venues, dear," Miss Pearl began, her pen poised over her notepad. "Now, we could use the town hall, but wouldn't it be just lovely to have the ceremony in the park under the magnolia tree? Imagine it, lanterns hanging from the branches."

Betty cut in, waving a handful of fabric swatches under Evie's nose. "But if you go with the park, you'll need to coordinate the colors with the scenery. I'm thinking a deep green with ivory accents."

Ruby, who had already filled half a page with notes, nodded sagely. "And don't forget about the logistics! We'll need to rent chairs, set up a sound system for the music... Oh, and we'll have to check the forecast, imagine if it rained! Maybe we should rent a tent, just in case?"

Grayson cleared his throat, trying to interject. "That's all very thoughtful, ladies, but Evie and I haven't even decided on a date yet, let alone the venue..."

Hattie, who had been scrolling through wedding playlists on her phone, glanced up with a raised eyebrow. "Oh, come on, Grayson, you know how things work around here. If we don't get started on the details, you'll end up with the church choir singing off-key and mismatched napkins."

Evie bit back a smile, nudging Grayson with her elbow. "You have to admit, they've got a point. We might as well let them run with it."

Grayson sighed, running a hand through his hair. "All right, all right. But can we at least talk about the food before we decide on the napkin colors?"

Later that afternoon, Evie and Grayson found themselves at the local bakery, where Helen, the town's most enthusiastic baker, awaited them with a sketchbook and a determined glint in her eye. The walls of the bakery were lined with display cakes, each more elaborate than the last, and the air was sweet with the scent of vanilla and sugar.

Helen ushered them to a small table, flipping open her sketchbook to reveal a drawing of a towering cake adorned with intricate sugar magnolias. "Now, I know you two said you wanted something simple, but I think we need to go *big* for this wedding. Just imagine, a six-tiered masterpiece inspired by the magnolia tree in the town square. It'll be the talk of the entire county!"

Grayson blanched, eyeing the sketch with a mixture of awe and trepidation. "Uh, Helen, we were thinking maybe something a little… smaller? More down-to-earth?"

Helen waved her hand dismissively, already flipping to a new page. "Nonsense! This is your one and only wedding cake, Grayson. You can't think small! Besides, a big cake will put Magnolia Springs on the map. People will travel from miles around just to see it!"

Evie shot Grayson an amused look, her hand covering her mouth as she tried not to laugh. "Maybe we can find a happy medium, Helen? How about three tiers, and we'll keep the sugar flowers? That way, it's still special, but not… you know, *monumental*."

Helen sighed dramatically but relented, jotting down Evie's suggestion with a flourish. "Fine, fine, I suppose I can work with that. But don't come crying to me when people say they were expecting more!"

The next stop on their wedding planning tour took them to a nearby boutique, where Clara and Sadie met up with Evie for some dress shopping. Grayson was conveniently left to fend for himself at the hardware store, though he seemed more than relieved to have a break from the whirlwind.

The boutique was small but filled with racks of white lace and satin, and Clara immediately took charge, bustling from one dress to the next with the enthusiasm of a kid in a candy store. Sadie, ever the fashion critic, trailed behind, offering her opinions with an air of authority.

"Now, Evie, you want something that really makes you *stand out*," Clara said, draping a veil over her head and spinning around dramatically. "Something like this, oh, I can see it now! You walking down the aisle, the whole town holding their breath—"

Sadie interrupted, shaking her head. "Clara, that veil is practically blinding. Evie needs something more classic, timeless, like this one." She held up a sleek, simple gown with a scooped neckline. "It's elegant, it's understated..."

Evie watched the two of them with a bemused smile, trying on dress after dress while they debated the merits of each one. But eventually, she found *the* dress, a delicate lace gown that fit her like a dream, with just the right touch of sparkle to make her feel like a bride. She turned in front of the mirror, her heart swelling as she imagined walking down the aisle toward Grayson.

She kept the dress a secret, though, asking Clara and Sadie not to tell a soul. After all, she wanted at least one part of the wedding to be a surprise.

By the time the day wound down, Evie and Grayson found themselves back at Iris & Ivy, sitting together on the back steps and watching the stars twinkle like a million diamonds. Evie leaned her head against Grayson's shoulder, her fingers playing with the edge of her scarf as she let out a contented sigh.

"I think we've made more decisions today than we have in the entire time we've been together," she said with a laugh, her breath puffing in the cold air.

Grayson wrapped an arm around her, pulling her close. "I know it's been crazy, but... I hope you're having fun. I don't want this to feel like a chore, Evie. I want it to be special for you."

Evie turned her head to look up at him, her eyes shining with affection. "It is special, Grayson. Because it's ours. And even if Miss Pearl and everyone else have a hand in it, at the end of the day, all I care about is you."

Grayson smiled, pressing a kiss to the top of her head. "I feel the same way, Evie. Whatever happens, I just want to be married to you."

They sat in silence for a while, knowing that the path ahead might be full of surprises, but it was a path they'd walk hand in hand, every step of the way.

Evie and Grayson lingered on the back steps of Iris & Ivy, wrapped in the quiet of the evening. The chaos of the day was behind them, and for a few precious moments, it was just the two of them, cocooned in a world that felt entirely their own. Evie rested her head against Grayson's shoulder, her heart full and her mind buzzing with the events of the day.

Grayson's voice broke the silence, soft and low. "You know, I never imagined planning a wedding would be quite like this. I always thought it was just picking a date and a place and, you know, showing up." He chuckled, shaking his head. "Turns out there's a lot more to it."

Evie laughed, the sound warm against the cold night air. "Welcome to the world of wedding planning, Grayson. And with Miss Pearl in charge, you should have known it wouldn't be that simple."

Grayson turned his head, pressing a gentle kiss to her temple. "I should've known better, huh? But as long as you're happy, I can handle a few extra opinions. Even if it means I have to survive Helen's cake-tasting sessions."

Evie smiled up at him, her expression turning tender. "I appreciate that you're trying so hard to make this special for me, Grayson. But you don't have to worry so much. As long as we're in this together, I know it's going to be perfect."

Grayson's gaze softened, his thumb brushing over the back of her hand. "I just want it to feel like *us*, you know? I want you to look back on this day and remember how much I love you, how much I want to build a life with you."

Evie's heart squeezed at his words, and she leaned up to kiss him, her lips brushing softly against his. "I already know, Grayson. And I feel the same way."

They stayed like that for a while, wrapped up in each other and the quiet magic of the evening. Evie closed her eyes, letting herself soak in the warmth of Grayson's embrace and the feeling of being right where she belonged.

The next morning, Evie and Grayson found themselves at yet another impromptu wedding planning session, this time, at Helen's bakery for a cake-tasting. Helen was in rare form, bustling around the kitchen with a determined look in her eye, her apron dusted with flour. She had prepared no fewer than six sample cakes for them to try, each one more elaborate than the last.

"Now, I know you two said you wanted something simple," Helen said, her tone suggesting that she didn't quite believe them, "but I think you'll change your mind once you taste this raspberry champagne cake. It's divine, if I do say so myself."

Evie and Grayson exchanged a look as they each picked up a fork and tried a bite of the cake. It was, as promised, delicious, but the towering design Helen had sketched out was far more extravagant than anything they'd imagined.

"This is amazing, Helen," Evie said diplomatically, wiping a crumb from the corner of her mouth. "But, um, maybe we could tone down the decorations a little? We don't want the cake to outshine the bride, after all."

Helen pursed her lips, considering this as if it were a personal affront to her artistic vision. "Well, I suppose we could do something a bit more... understated. But don't come crying to me if people say they were expecting more!"

Grayson chuckled, holding up his hands in surrender. "No complaints here, Helen. We trust you to make something beautiful, we just don't want it to topple over during the first dance."

Helen finally relented, her expression softening as she made a note in her sketchbook. "All right, I'll try to keep it down to three tiers and magnolias."

The rest of the week flew by in a blur of wedding-related activities. Clara and Sadie, true to their word, dragged Evie to every bridal shop within a fifty-mile radius, insisting that she try on veils, shoes, and accessories until she was nearly dizzy with lace and satin.

In between, Grayson found himself fielding questions from curious townsfolk, each one more eager than the last to find out the details of their upcoming nuptials. He couldn't even walk down Main Street without someone stopping him to offer advice or share a story about their own wedding.

"Just remember, son," old Mr. Thompson told him outside the hardware store, clapping a hand on his shoulder. "The trick is to just nod and agree with whatever she wants. It's her big day, after all."

Grayson smiled politely, though he couldn't help but think that it was just as much his day as Evie's. But he kept those thoughts to himself, knowing that the town was invested in their wedding in a way that only Magnolia Springs could be.

One evening, after a particularly exhausting food tastings, dress fittings, and venue discussions, Evie and Grayson found themselves back in her apartment, sitting on the couch with a blanket draped over their laps. A fire crackled in the small wood stove, casting a warm glow over the room.

Evie rested her head on Grayson's shoulder, letting out a long breath. "It's a lot, isn't it? I never realized how many little details there are to think about. And everyone has an opinion."

Grayson slipped an arm around her, pulling her closer. "Yeah, it's a lot. But you know what? I wouldn't trade it for anything. Because every time I see you get excited about some new idea, or when you find that little detail that makes you light up... it makes all the chaos worth it."

Evie smiled, closing her eyes as she snuggled against him. "You always know just what to say, don't you, Grayson Bennett?"

He pressed a kiss to the top of her head, his voice turning softer. "I just want you to know that, no matter what happens with this wedding, all I care about is standing up there with you, saying 'I do.' Everything else is just background noise."

Evie's heart swelled with love for him, and she tilted her head to meet his gaze, her eyes shining. "I feel the same way. And no matter what else happens, at least we'll have each other."

They sat together in the quiet of the evening, the fire crackling softly. And as Evie thought about all the twists and turns that had brought her to this moment, this life that she was building with Grayson, she knew that whatever challenges lay ahead, she wouldn't have it any other way.

Chapter 25

The morning dawned crisp and cold, with a pale winter sun casting long shadows over the town square. Grayson stood in the park, hands on his hips, surveying the pile of lumber that was soon to become the arbor for the wedding. Well, that was the plan, anyway. He'd enlisted the help of a few locals, Frank, the retired carpenter who swore he still had the best eye for design, and Sam, the hardware store clerk who was full of enthusiasm but short on experience.

Grayson glanced at Frank, who was peering at a set of blueprints through his reading glasses. "So, Frank, you think we can have this up by tomorrow?"

Frank adjusted his glasses, squinting at the plans. "Oh, sure, Grayson, we'll have it done in no time. I've built plenty of these things back in the day. Though, uh, I might make a few adjustments, just to give it a little more... character."

Grayson raised an eyebrow, trying to suppress a sense of foreboding. "Adjustments? What kind of adjustments?"

"Oh, you know," Frank said with a dismissive wave, "just a few decorative touches. You'll see. Trust me."

Before Grayson could respond, Sam trotted over with a hammer in one hand and a handful of nails in the other. "Hey, Grayson, do you think it's a problem that we're missing a couple of beams? Frank said he's got some old barn wood he can use instead."

Grayson rubbed the back of his neck, glancing between the enthusiastic Sam and the stubborn Frank. He was starting to think that building this arbor might require more than just a couple of helping hands. But before he could voice his concerns, Frank clapped him on the back.

"Don't worry, son, we've got this under control. You just keep the missus happy and leave the heavy lifting to us."

Grayson offered a hesitant smile, hoping that the final product would look something like the elegant arbor he and Evie had imagined. But a few hours later, when Miss Pearl arrived to inspect their progress, it was clear that things hadn't gone according to plan.

She stared at the structure, one side of which leaned at a precarious angle, and folded her arms across her chest. "Well, Grayson, it certainly has... character, I'll give you that. But are you sure it's supposed to look like it's about to fall over?"

Grayson grimaced, running a hand through his hair. "It's a work in progress, Miss Pearl. We've got it under control."

Miss Pearl gave him a skeptical look, then tapped one of the beams with her cane. To Grayson's horror, the entire structure shuddered, then collapsed in a heap of wood and nails with a resounding crash. Frank and Sam rushed over, looking equally stunned, while Miss Pearl tried to hide a smirk behind her hand.

"Well, I suppose that's one way to make an impression," she said dryly. "Maybe we'll need to rethink this arbor idea, hmm?"

Grayson sighed, rubbing his temples. "Yeah, maybe we should."

Meanwhile, over at *Iris & Ivy*, Evie was having her own struggles with the flower arrangements. Ruby had arrived early that morning, armed with an entire truckload of vibrant red roses that she insisted would be perfect for the wedding. Evie, however, had her heart set on magnolias, something simple and elegant to match the town's namesake.

"Now, Evie, I know you think magnolias are the way to go," Ruby said, gesturing toward the towering bouquets of roses she'd set up in the shop, "but look at these beauties! They'll add a pop of color, a little *zing* to your big day!"

Evie tried to be diplomatic, but she couldn't help the frown that tugged at her lips. "They're beautiful, Ruby, but I was really hoping for something more classic, you know? The magnolias just feel... right."

Clara, who had stopped by to help, glanced between the two women, clearly sensing the tension. "Uh, maybe we can find a compromise? What if we use the magnolias for the ceremony and the roses for the reception? That way, we get the best of both worlds?"

Sadie, who had been inspecting a particularly thorny rose, chimed in. "Or you could just do a mix of everything. A little chaos never hurt anyone, right? It'll be eclectic, like Magnolia Springs itself!"

Ruby pursed her lips, looking unconvinced, while Evie massaged her temples. "I appreciate the suggestions, you two, but I think..."

Before she could finish, the door swung open, and Helen from the bakery burst in, carrying a tray of cake samples. "I hope I'm not interrupting, but I brought the latest batch of frosting! We're going to need to taste-test these, oh, are those roses? Gorgeous! But, Evie, you *have* to see the sugar magnolias I've been working on. They'll match perfectly with—"

Evie held up her hands, trying to stave off the chaos. "Okay, okay! One thing at a time! Ruby, let's talk about the flowers again later, okay? And Helen, thank you, but I think I'll need another coffee before I can handle another round of cake."

Clara and Sadie exchanged amused looks, clearly enjoying the spectacle, while Ruby sighed and began packing up the roses. "All right, but I'm not giving up yet. You'll see—those roses would have been a hit."

Evie offered her a weary smile, feeling like she'd just survived a round of negotiations with a particularly stubborn committee. As much as she loved the support from her friends, she was starting to understand why people eloped.

That evening, the chaos continued at the rehearsal dinner, which Grayson had managed to organize at the town diner. The small space was packed with friends, family, and nearly half of the Match Making Club, all eager to share their well-wishes (and opinions) about the upcoming wedding. Grayson's best man, Derek, had flown in from out of state and immediately took it upon himself to organize a surprise "roast" of the groom.

Derek clinked a spoon against his glass, grinning as he stood up to address the crowd. "All right, folks, listen up! I've known Grayson since high school, so I've got a few stories to share about our favorite soon-to-be-married man."

Grayson groaned, sinking down in his chair as Evie shot him a sympathetic smile. "You didn't tell me your best man was a comedian," she whispered, squeezing his hand under the table.

Derek launched into a series of embarrassing anecdotes about Grayson's high school days, including a particularly memorable incident involving a failed attempt to ask out a girl to prom and a run-in with a malfunctioning lawnmower. The crowd roared with laughter, and even Miss Pearl had to wipe a tear from her eye as Derek mimed Grayson's frantic efforts to rescue his yard.

Grayson covered his face with his hands, shaking his head as Derek wrapped up the roast with a grin. "But in all seriousness, folks, Grayson's a good man, and I know he and Evie are going to be great together. So let's raise a glass to them, may your life together be filled with love, laughter, and fewer lawnmower incidents."

The toast was met with a round of applause, and Grayson managed to smile as he clinked glasses with Evie, who leaned in to kiss his cheek. "Don't worry," she whispered, "I'll still marry you, even if you do have a talent for getting into trouble."

After the dinner wound down and the guests finally left, Evie and Grayson stepped outside into the chilly night air, grateful for the quiet after the noise and laughter of the evening. They walked hand in hand down Main Street, until they reached the gazebo in the town park.

Evie turned to face Grayson, her breath fogging in the cold. "You know, for all the craziness, I wouldn't trade any of this. I've never laughed so much in my life."

Grayson wrapped his arms around her, pulling her close. "Me neither. And as long as we're laughing, I think we'll be okay. Even if that arbor never gets built."

Evie laughed, resting her head against his chest. "As long as I have you, I don't care where we say our vows. But I have to admit, I'm kind of looking forward to what Miss Pearl has planned next."

Grayson groaned, but his smile was fond as he pressed a kiss to her forehead. "As long as it doesn't involve any more surprise roasts, I'll take whatever comes."

They stood together under the twinkling lights of the gazebo, sharing a kiss that held all the promises they'd made and all the hope for their future. And even though the road to their wedding was full of bumps and misadventures, they knew that every step had brought them closer to each other, and that was all that mattered.

Later that night, Miss Pearl gathered with Ruby, Betty, and Hattie in her living room, each of them armed with a notebook and a cup of tea. They reviewed the events of the rehearsal dinner with an air of satisfied accomplishment, already plotting how to make the wedding day even more memorable.

"Well, ladies," Miss Pearl said, raising her teacup with a wink, "I think it's safe to say that Grayson and Evie are ready for whatever comes next. But just in case, I've got a few more tricks up my sleeve."

Betty nodded, a conspiratorial smile spreading across her face. "Of course you do, Miss Pearl. And we wouldn't have it any other way."

Chapter 26

The first light of dawn crept through the curtains of Evie's apartment, painting the room in a gentle golden hue. Evie lay in bed for a moment, staring up at the ceiling as the reality of the day washed over her. It was her wedding day, the day she would marry Grayson, the man who had turned her world upside down in the most beautiful way. Her heart fluttered with a mix of excitement and nerves, the anticipation bubbling up inside her like a shaken-up bottle of champagne.

Before she could collect her thoughts, there was a knock at her door, followed by Clara and Sadie's familiar voices. They sounded as excited as a couple of kids on Christmas morning. "Evie, open up! We've got mimosas, and we're ready to make you look like a bride!"

Evie chuckled, pulling on her robe and shuffling to the door. As soon as she opened it, Clara and Sadie barreled inside, each holding a bottle of orange juice and champagne. They wore matching "Bride Squad" t-shirts, and Clara had even added a glittery veil to her ensemble.

"Good morning, almost-Mrs. Bennett!" Clara sang out, handing Evie a glass filled to the brim with bubbly. "How are you feeling? Ready to become a married woman?"

Evie took a sip, savoring the sweetness of the champagne and the warmth of her friends' presence. "I'm excited... and nervous. But mostly excited. I just can't believe today is finally here."

Sadie flopped down on the bed, grinning as she popped the cap off another bottle. "Well, you'd better believe it, because we've got a lot to do! And if we're going to get through it, we need a little liquid courage."

Clara winked, raising her glass in a toast. "Here's to Evie and Grayson, to a day full of love, laughter, and no wardrobe malfunctions!"

Evie laughed, clinking her glass against Clara's. "I'll drink to that."

As they sipped their mimosas, gave each other facials, polished nails, did each other's hair and then helped Evie into her wedding dress, Clara and Sadie regaled her with stories about weddings gone wrong, dresses that ripped, cakes that toppled over, and, in one memorable instance, a ring-bearing dog that got loose during the ceremony.

"But don't worry," Clara said with a wink as she adjusted the lace of Evie's veil, "we've made sure everything's going to be perfect for you. And even if something does go wrong, just remember, you're still marrying the man of your dreams, and that's all that matters."

Evie smiled at her friends, her heart swelling with gratitude. "Thank you, both of you. I couldn't have done any of this without you."

Sadie waved her hand dismissively, but her eyes were misty. "Oh, stop it, you're going to make me cry before we even get to the ceremony. Now, let's get you ready to go meet your groom!"

Across town, Grayson stood in the hardware store, pacing back and forth between the aisles. He tried to focus on breathing, but his nerves had other plans. His groomsmen, Derek and Sam, lounged against the counter, sipping coffee and offering what they clearly thought were words of wisdom.

"Just remember, Grayson," Derek said with a smirk, "as long as you don't trip walking down the aisle, you'll be fine. Oh, and don't forget to smile during the photos. You always look like you're about to sneeze in pictures."

Grayson shot him a look, half amused, half exasperated. "Thanks, Derek. Real helpful."

Sam nodded sagely, slapping Grayson on the back. "Seriously, though, don't worry. Evie loves you, and that's all you need to remember. Plus, Miss Pearl's got everything planned down to the minute. There's no way this wedding won't be perfect."

Grayson let out a breath, trying to focus on those words. But just as he was starting to feel a little more settled, the bell over the store's door jangled, and in walked Miss Pearl herself, looking every bit like a general inspecting her troops.

"Morning, Grayson!" she chirped, adjusting the brooch on her lapel. "I just thought I'd stop by and see how you're holding up. And to remind you not to forget the rings! You know, I heard a story once about a groom who left the rings in his fishing tackle box, imagine that!"

Grayson patted the pocket of his jacket, where the ring box rested safely. "I've got them right here, Miss Pearl. Don't worry."

Miss Pearl beamed, giving him an approving nod. "Good boy. Now, just remember to take a deep breath and enjoy the day. It's going to be beautiful, I've made sure of it!"

With that, she left the store, leaving Grayson with a mixture of amusement and gratitude. He glanced at Derek and Sam, who both looked like they were trying not to laugh, and rolled his eyes. "All right, boys, let's go get me married."

As the guests gathered in the town park, Miss Pearl and her friends bustled around, ensuring every detail was in place. Ruby's flower arrangements, despite the earlier disagreements, turned out beautifully, with magnolias and roses artfully woven together into elegant bouquets that lined the aisle. Helen's towering cake stood proudly under a tent, adorned with sugar magnolias that shimmered in the winter sunlight.

Evie arrived with Clara and Sadie, the gazebo where she and Grayson would exchange their vows was draped in twinkling lights and garlands of greenery. It was more magical than she'd ever imagined.

Miss Pearl hurried over, dabbing at her eyes with a lace handkerchief. "Oh, Evie, you look absolutely stunning, dear! Grayson won't know what hit him when he sees you walking down that aisle."

Evie's smile wobbled, her nerves suddenly kicking in. "Thank you, Miss Pearl. I just... I hope everything goes smoothly."

Miss Pearl patted her hand, her eyes twinkling. "Don't you worry, dear. Even if there's a little hiccup or two, you'll look back on this day and laugh. Now, go take your place, and let's get this wedding started!"

When the music began to play, and Evie stepped out into the aisle, every worry and nervous thought melted away. All she could see was Grayson, standing at the end of the aisle with a look in his eyes that made her heart skip a beat. As she walked toward him, arm in arm with her uncle Frank, she couldn't help but think of all the moments that had brought them here, every misadventure, every shared laugh, every secret smile.

Grayson's breath caught when he saw her, his hand tightening around the ring box in his pocket. She looked like a vision, her smile radiant beneath the veil, and he felt a lump rise in his throat. How had he gotten so lucky?

As she reached the gazebo, Grayson took her hand, his voice soft as he whispered, "You're beautiful."

Evie squeezed his hand, her eyes shining with unshed tears. "So are you."

The ceremony passed in a blur of joy and emotion, with Grayson and Evie exchanging vows that spoke to the journey they'd taken together. When it was Grayson's turn, his voice cracked with emotion as he promised to love Evie through every season of their lives.

Evie's vows were just as heartfelt, and by the time they exchanged rings, there wasn't a dry eye in the park. Even Miss Pearl sniffled quietly in the back row, dabbing at her cheeks and whispering to Ruby, "I knew they were meant to be, from the very first day."

As Grayson and Evie shared their first kiss as husband and wife, the crowd erupted into applause, their cheers echoing through the park. And for a moment, the world seemed to hold its breath, suspended in a perfect moment of happiness.

They broke apart, breathless and grinning, their hands still intertwined as they turned to face the people who had made this day possible. Grayson leaned close, whispering in Evie's ear, "I've never been happier in my life."

Evie turned to him, her smile soft and filled with love. "Me neither, Grayson. This is everything I ever dreamed of."

As the guests gathered around to offer their congratulations, Miss Pearl sidled up to them, her smile smug and satisfied. "Well, I'd say this was a success, wouldn't you?"

Grayson grinned, wrapping an arm around Evie's waist. "We couldn't have done it without you, Miss Pearl. Thank you, for everything."

Miss Pearl waved a hand, but her eyes shone with pride. "Oh, don't thank me yet. There's still a reception to get through, and I've got a few more surprises up my sleeve."

Evie and Grayson exchanged a look, both laughing as they followed Miss Pearl toward the reception tent. Whatever came next, they knew they could handle it, together.

Chapter 27

The wedding reception was in full swing under the twinkling lights of the reception tent, laughter and music filling the air. Guests mingled around the tables, sipping on hot cider and champagne while a bluegrass band played lively tunes in the corner. The scent of freshly cut pine and cinnamon candles blended with the sweetness of the wedding cake, and the warmth of the heaters kept the winter chill at bay.

Evie and Grayson had already shared their first slice of cake, both managing to get frosting on each other's noses amid the laughter and cheers. They clinked glasses with well-wishers, each toasting to a lifetime of love and happiness. As the guests continued to enjoy the evening, Evie caught sight of Miss Pearl standing at the back of the tent, her arms crossed and a knowing smile playing at the corners of her mouth.

Evie couldn't help but chuckle, shaking her head slightly as she adjusted her grip on the bouquet she held. Miss Pearl had hinted more than once about making sure the bouquet ended up in the right hands, and now that the moment had arrived, Evie couldn't resist playing along with her plan.

She glanced back at the group of women gathered behind her, all eagerly anticipating the toss. Clara and Ruby were at the front, jostling for position, while Sadie lingered at the very back, clearly hoping to avoid the whole spectacle. Evie's eyes met Miss Pearl's, and Miss Pearl gave her a wink, her grin widening.

Evie turned around, facing away from the crowd, and took a deep breath. With a dramatic flourish, she tossed the bouquet over her shoulder, sending it soaring through the air. The cluster of women reached up with hopeful hands, but the bouquet arced gracefully past them all and landed squarely in Sadie's grasp.

Sadie's eyes widened, her mouth forming a perfect "O" of surprise as she stared down at the bouquet in her hands. It took her a moment to realize what had just happened, and by the time she did, the entire crowd had erupted into cheers and laughter.

"Well, well, well!" Clara called out, clapping her hands. "Looks like fate has other plans for you, Sadie!"

Sadie flushed crimson, glancing over her shoulder as if she might escape through the back of the tent. But before she could make a break for it, Miss Pearl appeared behind her, gently but firmly guiding her back toward the center of the room.

"Now, now, Sadie, no slipping out early," Miss Pearl said with a mischievous smile. "You caught the bouquet fair and square, and you know what that means!"

Sadie shot her a pleading look, but Miss Pearl merely patted her shoulder and pushed her back toward the front of the crowd. The guests laughed and cheered, clapping Sadie on the back as she made her way forward, looking like a deer caught in headlights.

Meanwhile, Grayson took his place on the other side of the room, the garter in his hand. He cast a playful look in Evie's direction before turning back to the gathered group of single men. Wyatt stood near the back, chatting with one of the groomsmen and clearly not paying much attention to the proceedings.

Grayson grinned, wound up his arm, and launched the garter into the air. It sailed across the room in a high arc, and just as Wyatt turned around, it smacked him right in the face before dropping neatly into the glass of champagne he was holding.

The crowd roared with laughter, and Wyatt blinked in confusion, looking down at the garter that floated in his drink. He plucked it out, holding it up with a bemused expression as his friends clapped him on the back.

"Looks like you're next, Wyatt!" someone called out, and the guests laughed and cheered, urging him forward.

Wyatt's cheeks flushed a deep red, and he glanced across the room to where Sadie was standing with the bouquet still clutched in her hands. Sadie shot him a wide-eyed look that spoke volumes *How did we end up in this mess?* and he offered her a sheepish shrug in return.

Grayson, clearly enjoying the spectacle, held up a hand to quiet the crowd. "All right, folks, it's time for the next tradition! Sadie and Wyatt, you've got to join us on the dance floor after Evie and I share our first dance."

Sadie looked like she might protest, but before she could make a move, Miss Pearl was already steering her toward the dance floor, her grip firm and her smile unyielding. "Oh no, Sadie dear, no backing out now! You caught that bouquet for a reason, and I'd say it's about time you and Wyatt had a little dance, don't you think?"

Sadie shot Miss Pearl a glare that might have withered a lesser woman, but Miss Pearl remained as unflappable as ever, practically pushing her onto the dance floor. Wyatt stood waiting, his face flushed and his hands shoved awkwardly into his pockets, clearly unsure of what to do next.

The band struck up a slow tune, and Grayson led Evie to the center of the floor for their first dance as husband and wife. The crowd gathered around, watching with misty eyes as the newlyweds swayed together, wrapped up in each other and the magic of the moment. Evie rested her head against Grayson's chest, smiling as she listened to the steady rhythm of his heartbeat.

"Did you see the look on Sadie's face?" she whispered, her shoulders shaking with quiet laughter. "I think she might actually strangle Miss Pearl when this is over."

Grayson chuckled, pressing a kiss to the top of her head. "She's probably already plotting her escape route. But, you know, I think Miss Pearl might be onto something. Sadie and Wyatt... they'd make a good pair."

Evie glanced over at the edge of the dance floor, where Miss Pearl was watching them with a proud smile. "Well, if anyone can make it happen, it's Miss Pearl. And you know what? I'm glad she meddled. Without her, I might never have found you."

Grayson's smile softened, and he pulled her closer, their movements slowing as they danced. "I'm grateful for that too, Evie. And for everything that brought us here."

As the song drew to a close, the guests clapped and cheered, and Grayson dipped Evie low before planting a playful kiss on her lips. They both laughed as they straightened, breathless and happy.

The band began to play a new tune, and the crowd turned their attention to Sadie and Wyatt, who stood awkwardly at the edge of the dance floor. Wyatt rubbed the back of his neck, glancing around as if hoping for a distraction, while Sadie looked like she might bolt at any moment.

But Miss Pearl was having none of it. With a surprisingly strong grip, she nudged Sadie forward and called out, "Come on now, you two! It's just a little dance, let's see what you've got!"

The guests cheered them on, clapping and whistling until Wyatt finally stepped forward, offering Sadie his hand with a shy, tentative smile. "Well, I guess we'd better get this over with, huh?"

Sadie sighed, but a reluctant smile tugged at her lips as she placed her hand in his. "Yeah, I guess so."

Wyatt chuckled, his expression softening as he pulled her into a slow, swaying rhythm. "Don't worry, Sadie. I won't bite."

Sadie's face turned beet red at Wyatt's comment. As the two of them began to dance, the guests broke into applause once more, clearly delighted by the unexpected pairing. Miss Pearl watched from the sidelines, a satisfied smile curving her lips as she leaned over to Ruby and whispered, "You know, I have a good feeling about those two. Just you wait, there's a spark there, even if they don't know it yet."

Ruby nodded, her eyes twinkling. "Well, if anyone can make them see it, it's you, Miss Pearl. Now, let's get back to celebrating before Sadie realizes what you're up to."

Miss Pearl's laughter mingled with the music as she joined the other guests, her heart full as she watched the bride and groom, her most successful matchmaking project yet, sharing a dance that marked the beginning of their new life together.

And in the corner of the dance floor, where a nervous Sadie and an awkward Wyatt moved tentatively in each other's arms, the seeds of another love story were just beginning to take root.

Chapter 28

The dance floor swayed under the weight of laughter and celebration as Sadie and Wyatt stepped gingerly into the spotlight. The band played a slow tune, and despite the romantic setting, the atmosphere between them was anything but smooth. As they swayed together, it quickly became clear to everyone watching that both were as nervous as a couple of cats in a room full of rocking chairs.

Sadie glanced up at Wyatt, her cheeks flushed pink as she attempted to steady her breathing. "So... um, how's the weather been treating you?" she asked, clearly struggling to find a starting point for their conversation. It was a classic fallback question, but it felt entirely inadequate in the midst of such a moment.

Wyatt scratched the back of his head, his eyes darting to the floor as he shuffled his feet. "Uh, it's been pretty cold, I guess. But I mean, it is winter, right? That's what you expect." His awkward grin didn't quite hide the anxiety bubbling beneath the surface.

Sadie nodded, the silence stretching between them like a tightrope. "Right, yes. Winter. Cold. Fun stuff." She forced a laugh, but it felt more like a hiccup than anything genuinely funny. They both stood there, shifting on their feet, unsure of what to say next.

"So, uh, have you been keeping busy?" Wyatt tried, his voice faltering a bit. How's the store doing?"

Sadie's expression brightened slightly at the mention of the store, her comfort zone. "Yeah, I have! I.ve had a busy week.

"That's great," Wyatt said, "I mean, hope the store is doing well."

Sadie grinned, grateful for the shift in conversation, however slight. "It's is and... maybe you should stop by more often, you know to talk or whatever."

"I'd like that." Wyatt replied, his nerves slowly easing as he caught her eye. "Maybe I could take you to out for coffee? You know, to celebrate you catching the bouquet." Wyatt said with a warm smile.

Sadie blinked, caught off guard by the sudden invitation. "Oh, wow, really? I mean, I thought you might be too busy. You know, with your family's farm and everything."

"Nah, I can make time for coffee and a little chat," he said, chuckling lightly. He gave her a lopsided smile, and for a moment, the tension faded.

As they danced, a tentative rhythm developed, their bodies swaying in sync as they talked. Sadie found herself easing into the moment, enjoying the chance to connect without the pressure of being "on display."

The conversation felt lighter, and they both relaxed just a little more. However, just as Sadie was starting to enjoy their banter, a stray thought crossed her mind: *What if this was just a friendly outing?*

"Do you really think they're a good match?" Sadie asked, her voice dropping a bit, her curiosity getting the better of her. "Evie and Grayson, I mean."

Wyatt's expression shifted slightly, and he hesitated before responding. "I think so. They complement each other really well, you know? It's like they each bring out the best in the other. I mean, look at how happy they are tonight."

Sadie nodded, feeling a small pang of longing at his words. "Yeah, I get that. They really do seem perfect together."

A moment of silence hung between them, thick with unspoken thoughts. Sadie felt the familiar flutter of attraction she had tried to ignore since their last encounter. She glanced up at Wyatt, who was also clearly struggling with his own feelings, the warmth in his cheeks betraying his nervousness.

"Sadie, can I ask you something?" Wyatt's voice was serious, his gaze searching hers. "Do you ever think about... well, relationships? You know, beyond just friendships?"

Sadie felt her heart race, a mix of excitement and apprehension coursing through her. "Uh, yeah. Sometimes. I mean, I've thought about it. But it's complicated, isn't it?" She searched his face, trying to gauge where this conversation was headed.

Wyatt nodded slowly, his brow furrowing as he spoke. "Complicated? I've always liked you, Sadie. But I wasn't sure if you'd be interested in anything more. You know, with everything going on in town."

Sadie's stomach flipped, and for a moment, the music and the guests faded into the background. "Wyatt, I—"

Before she could finish, the song shifted, and the crowd erupted into applause, drawing attention away from their conversation. Grayson and Evie, now standing hand in hand at the edge of the dance floor, beckoned them over.

"Hey, you two lovebirds!" Evie called, her voice bubbling with excitement. "Come on, join us for a group dance!"

Sadie shot Wyatt a look, and they both nodded, returning to the present. The moment had slipped through their fingers, but the spark of attraction lingered, teasing at the edges of their awareness as they joined the throng of guests.

<hr>

As the group danced and laughed, the rest of the reception unfolded in a joyful haze, with Evie and Grayson leading the way. The energy in the room was infectious, and even Sadie and Wyatt found themselves swept up in the excitement, their earlier awkwardness fading as they joined in the laughter.

Miss Pearl watched the festivities from the sidelines, a satisfied grin on her face as she observed the evolving dynamics between Sadie and Wyatt. "Just you wait," she murmured to Ruby, "I have a feeling those two are going to surprise us all."

As the night continued, the music played on, and the newlyweds twirled around the dance floor, celebrating not just their love, but the love that was blossoming around them, something that Magnolia Springs seemed to do best.

Chapter 29

The reception was still buzzing with energy when the doors to the tent swung open, letting in a gust of cool night air. A tall, broad-shouldered man in a crisp military uniform stepped inside, his expression a mix of relief and determination. He scanned the room, his gaze landing on Evie, who was in the midst of a twirl on the dance floor with Grayson. A small, genuine smile tugged at the corner of his mouth as he watched his sister, clearly happy.

Evie caught sight of the newcomer just as Grayson spun her around again, and her face lit up with a mixture of joy and surprise. "Everett! You made it!" She broke away from Grayson, rushing across the room to throw her arms around her brother.

Everett Matthews, Evie's older brother, wrapped her in a tight hug, lifting her off the ground for a moment before setting her down gently. His dark hair, closely cropped in military style, contrasted with the warmth in his hazel eyes. He wore his uniform like a second skin, the fabric pressed and pristine, and his posture radiated a sense of discipline. But his smile softened when he looked at his sister.

"Of course I made it, kid," he said, his voice carrying the unmistakable cadence of someone used to giving orders. "I wouldn't miss your big day for the world, even if I had to hitch a ride from the airport."

Evie pulled back, tears shimmering in her eyes as she looked up at him. "You have no idea how much this means to me, Everett. I thought you were stuck overseas and wouldn't be able to make it."

Everett's expression grew serious for a moment, but he squeezed her shoulder gently. "I pulled a few strings and got some leave time. You deserve to have your family here, Evie. And I've got to meet this guy who thinks he's good enough to marry my little sister."

Evie laughed, glancing over her shoulder at Grayson, who approached with an easy smile. "Grayson, this is my brother, Everett. Everett, meet my husband."

Grayson extended his hand, and Everett shook it with a firm grip. "Good to meet you, Grayson. You've got a lot of people in this town who think pretty highly of you. Guess I'll find out if you're worth all the hype."

Grayson chuckled, meeting Everett's serious gaze with a steady one of his own. "I hope I live up to your expectations, Everett. And I promise to take good care of Evie."

Everett's expression softened, and he nodded. "That's all I can ask for. And, Grayson, thanks for making her happy. I haven't seen her smile like this in a long time."

Evie wiped away a stray tear, pulling both men into another hug. "All right, enough with the serious talk! It's a party, after all. Come on, Everett, you've got to meet everyone. I think Miss Pearl might even have a story or two to share with you."

It didn't take long for Everett to become the center of attention, with Miss Pearl leading the charge. She practically swooped in, taking him by the arm and guiding him to a quieter corner of the tent. "Everett, dear, it's so wonderful to finally meet you. Evie's told us so much about you, but I have a feeling there's more to the story. Tell me, how does a brave young man like you find his way back home?"

Everett chuckled, a hint of amusement in his eyes as he allowed Miss Pearl to steer the conversation. "Well, ma'am, I've been overseas for a while, but now that I'm back, I think I'll be sticking around for a bit. Besides, someone's got to make sure Evie doesn't get into too much trouble."

Miss Pearl's eyes gleamed with interest, her matchmaking instincts clearly kicking into high gear. "You know, Everett, a man like you shouldn't be alone in a town like this. Magnolia Springs has a way of bringing people together. In fact, I was just thinking about our dear Sadie..."

Everett raised an eyebrow, glancing over at the dance floor where Sadie stood chatting with Clara. "Sadie, huh? She seems nice, but I don't think she's looking for anything serious."

Miss Pearl patted his arm, her smile sly. "Oh, you'd be surprised, dear. Sometimes all it takes is the right nudge, and people find they have more in common than they thought. Why don't you ask her to dance? See where things go. You never know what might happen."

Everett hesitated, glancing over at Sadie again. She caught his eye briefly, her expression curious but not unkind. Finally, he let out a breath and nodded. "All right, Miss Pearl. I'll give it a shot."

Miss Pearl beamed, giving him an encouraging nudge toward the dance floor. "That's the spirit! Go on, now. Show her that military charm."

Sadie was in the middle of a conversation with Clara when Everett approached, his hands tucked casually into his pockets. He cleared his throat, drawing her attention, and offered her a small, tentative smile. "Hey, Sadie. Would you, uh, like to dance?"

Sadie blinked in surprise, glancing between Everett and Clara, who was grinning like a Cheshire cat. "Oh! Well, I... sure, I guess I could dance a little." She shot a suspicious look toward Miss Pearl, who stood off to the side with an all-too-innocent expression, and then turned back to Everett. "Why not?"

Clara gave her a playful nudge as she walked past, mouthing *go get 'em* before disappearing into the crowd. Sadie's cheeks flushed as she took Everett's outstretched hand, letting him lead her to the center of the dance floor.

The music shifted to a slower tune, and they began to sway to the rhythm, moving awkwardly at first. But as they found their footing, the tension eased, and Sadie even managed a small smile. "So, Everett, what brings you to Magnolia Springs? Other than the wedding, of course."

Everett chuckled, his grip on her hand gentle as he spun her in a slow circle. "Mostly the wedding. But I've been thinking it might be time for a change of pace. Figured I'd stick around for a bit, see if I can't help Evie out with a few things."

Sadie tilted her head, her curiosity piqued. "That's nice of you. She's really happy now. Grayson's a good guy."

"Yeah, I can see that," Everett replied, his voice thoughtful. "And it's nice to see her settled, you know? After all the things she's been through, I'm glad she's found someone who's good for her."

They fell into a comfortable silence, the music filling the space between them. Sadie found herself relaxing, letting the rhythm guide their movements. Everett's calm, steady presence was a welcome change from the usual whirlwind of emotions she felt around Wyatt. It wasn't that she didn't like Wyatt, far from it, but there was something different about dancing with Everett, something that made her feel like she could take a deep breath without overthinking every little detail.

"You're pretty good at this, Everett," Sadie remarked, her lips quirking into a playful smile. "Didn't expect a soldier to have moves."

Everett laughed, his eyes crinkling at the corners. "Oh, I wouldn't go that far. But I've picked up a few things over the years. You're not so bad yourself, Sadie."

She shrugged, a shy smile tugging at her lips. "Well, it helps when your dance partner isn't stepping on your toes every five seconds."

Across the dance floor, Wyatt leaned against the refreshment table, his arms crossed over his chest as he watched Sadie and Everett dance. His jaw was set, a hint of frustration flickering in his eyes as he took in the easy way they moved together. He knew he had no right to feel possessive, he and Sadie weren't anything official, but he couldn't shake the uncomfortable tightness in his chest as he watched them laugh together.

Clara appeared at his side, following his gaze with a knowing smirk. "You know, Wyatt, if you wanted to dance with Sadie so badly, you could've just asked her first."

Wyatt shot her a sidelong glance, his expression darkening slightly. "Yeah, well, I guess I missed my chance, didn't I?"

Clara shook her head, giving him a playful nudge with her elbow. "Come on, don't be such a sore loser. There's still time to make your move, you know."

Wyatt let out a low sigh, his gaze returning to Sadie and Everett. "Maybe. But something tells me it's going to be a lot harder than I thought."

As the song drew to a close, Sadie and Everett shared a polite smile, exchanging a few more pleasantries before parting ways. But as Sadie returned to the edge of the dance floor, she couldn't help but feel a strange mix of emotions swirling inside her, confusion, curiosity, and a hint of something she couldn't quite put her finger on.

And as Wyatt watched her from the sidelines, a new resolve settled in his chest. He wasn't going to let this opportunity slip away again, not without a fight.

Chapter 30

The small living room of Miss Pearl's cozy house was packed with the familiar faces of Magnolia Springs' most enthusiastic matchmakers. The air smelled faintly of lavender from the tea she had just brewed, and the fireplace crackled, casting a warm glow over the room. The curtains were drawn tight against the cold, and the winter sun filtered through just enough to bathe the group in a golden light.

Ruby, Betty, and Hattie sat around the coffee table, each clutching a steaming mug, while Clara lounged on the couch with a sly smile playing on her lips. Miss Pearl stood at the head of the room, her hands folded over her cane, her eyes twinkling with the excitement of a new challenge. It was a scene that had become almost a tradition in the town, Miss Pearl, leading the charge in yet another mission of the heart.

"Well, ladies," Miss Pearl began, her voice carrying an air of conspiratorial glee, "it looks like our job isn't quite done yet. The wedding was a great success, if I do say so myself, but there's another pair of lovebirds in desperate need of a little nudge. And I think you all know who I'm talking about."

Hattie leaned forward, her curiosity piqued. "You're talking about Sadie and Wyatt, aren't you? Oh, those two! They're like oil and water. I don't know how you're going to make that work, Miss Pearl."

Miss Pearl's smile widened, a glint in her eye. "Oh, I've seen that look in their eyes, Hattie. They can deny it all they want, but there's something there, something worth fighting for. And you know what they say: opposites attract."

Clara, who had been sipping her tea with a knowing smirk, set her cup down and leaned back, crossing her arms. "I'm in, Miss Pearl. I've seen the way Sadie looks at Wyatt when she thinks no one's watching. And with Everett around to shake things up, well... I think we can make a little magic happen."

Ruby and Betty exchanged a glance, then nodded in unison. "We're on board, too," Ruby said. "Sadie deserves to find someone who makes her happy, and Wyatt... well, he just needs a push in the right direction."

Miss Pearl clapped her hands together, her delight clear. "Wonderful! Now, let's get down to business. We've got two weeks before Sadie starts getting suspicious, and we need to make every moment count. Everett's already staying at Evie's place while she and Grayson settle into married life, and that gives us the perfect opportunity to work behind the scenes."

Betty raised a hand, her expression thoughtful. "So, what's the plan, exactly? How do we make sure they spend enough time together to let those sparks fly?"

Miss Pearl's smile turned mischievous as she outlined the strategy. "Step one: we get Everett to encourage Sadie to visit the flower shop more often, say, to help out while Evie's away. Clara grinned, her eyes twinkling. "And step two?"

Miss Pearl's voice lowered conspiratorially. "Step two involves a few 'accidental' run-ins around town. A New Year's Eve dance, maybe a bachelor's auction for the Church's fundraiser... situations that make it impossible for Sadie and Wyatt to avoid each other. With Everett keeping an eye on things, we'll have just the right amount of help without making it too obvious."

Hattie let out a delighted laugh, clapping her hands together. "Oh, Miss Pearl, you always think of everything! This is going to be even better than the time we set up that romantic weekend for Evie and Grayson."

Ruby smirked, taking another sip of her tea. "Remember how they both pretended it was a coincidence, but we all knew better? That was a work of art, if you ask me."

Miss Pearl nodded, her gaze drifting toward the window as if she could already see the results of their new plan unfolding. "Well, ladies, we've done good work in the past, but this one's going to take all our skills. Sadie and Wyatt will never see it coming. But when they finally do, they'll thank us for it."

Meanwhile, across town, Everett sat at the small kitchen table in Evie's apartment, going over the inventory for the flower shop. The morning sun streamed through the window, casting a soft light over the neatly stacked ledgers and vases filled with winter blooms. He glanced around the cozy space, the scent of Evie's favorite lavender candle lingering in the air, and couldn't help but feel a sense of calm settle over him.

The door creaked open, and Clara peeked her head inside, a wide grin on her face. "Hey, Everett, how's it going? Getting the hang of flower shop duty yet?"

Everett chuckled, pushing the paperwork aside. "It's not exactly my usual gig, but I think I'm managing. It's good to have something to do while I'm in town."

Clara sauntered inside, leaning against the counter as she shot him a sly look. "So, you're going to be in town for a bit, huh? You know, Sadie could use some help. Maybe you could convince her to stop by the shop when she's free."

Everett raised an eyebrow, catching on to her not-so-subtle suggestion. "Are you trying to play matchmaker, Clara? Because I think Miss Pearl's already got that covered."

Clara laughed, her smile bright and mischievous. "Let's just say we're all invested in seeing Sadie and Wyatt find some happiness. And you're in a perfect position to help out. Besides, from what I hear, you've got a knack for nudging people in the right direction."

Everett leaned back in his chair, a thoughtful expression crossing his face. "Maybe you're right. Sadie seems like she could use a little push. And, well, I wouldn't mind keeping an eye on Wyatt, either. He looks like he's got a lot on his mind."

Clara's grin widened. "Exactly! So, what do you say? Think you can handle being Miss Pearl's newest accomplice?"

Everett smirked, shaking his head. "Sure, why not? I've faced tougher missions, after all. And if it means seeing Sadie and Wyatt get their act together, I'm in."

Later that afternoon, as the sun began to set over Magnolia Springs, Miss Pearl gathered the Match Making Club for one final pep talk before sending everyone on their way. The atmosphere in her cozy living room was buzzing with excitement, the women exchanging excited whispers and making last-minute adjustments to their plan.

"Now remember, ladies," Miss Pearl said, raising her cane for emphasis, "this is a delicate operation. We can't push too hard, or they'll catch on. But with Everett keeping an eye on things at the flower shop, we'll have just the right amount of leverage to make sure everything goes smoothly."

Hattie giggled, leaning closer. "I can't wait to see Sadie's face when she starts realizing she has feelings for Wyatt. It's going to be priceless!"

Ruby nodded enthusiastically, adding, "And if Wyatt finally stops being so stubborn and just *talks* to her, I think they might actually have a chance."

Miss Pearl's smile was practically gleeful as she surveyed her team. "Well, then, let's make it happen. To Operation Sadie and Wyatt!"

The group raised their teacups in a toast, and Miss Pearl clinked hers against each one with a wink. "They'll never know what hit them."

As the winter evening sun set in, Everett found himself back at the flower shop, finishing up a few tasks for the day. The bell over the door jingled, and he looked up to see Sadie walking in, her cheeks pink from the cold. She gave him a shy smile, glancing around the shop.

"Hey, Everett. I thought I'd stop by and see if you needed any help... or, you know, company. The general store is pretty slow today."

Everett returned her smile, gesturing to a stack of new flower pots that needed organizing. "I'd appreciate the help, Sadie. And if you're up for it, I could use a second opinion on some of these displays."

Sadie's smile brightened, and she shrugged out of her coat, moving to join him by the workbench. As they worked side by side, the atmosphere was warm and easy, their earlier awkwardness replaced by a sense of camaraderie. Everett couldn't help but think that maybe, just maybe, Miss Pearl's plan was off to a good start.

Across town, Wyatt sat at his usual spot in the diner, nursing a cup of coffee and staring out the window. He couldn't shake the memory of seeing Sadie dancing with Everett, the way she'd smiled at him in a way she never seemed to smile at Wyatt. It gnawed at him, leaving a bitter taste in his mouth.

He didn't notice Clara slip into the seat across from him until she snapped her fingers in front of his face. "Earth to Wyatt! You look like someone stole your favorite hunting spot."

Wyatt blinked, snapping out of his thoughts, and gave Clara a half-hearted smile. "Sorry, Clara. Just... got a lot on my mind."

Clara leaned forward, resting her chin in her hand as she studied him with a knowing look. "Let me guess, it has something to do with a certain cute little brunette who caught the bouquet at the wedding?"

Wyatt's jaw clenched, but he couldn't deny the truth. "I just don't get it, Clara. I thought maybe... I don't know. Maybe she'd look at me the way she looks at Everett."

Clara's smile softened, and she reached out to pat his hand. "Oh, Wyatt, you big dummy. Sadie's just as confused as you are. She doesn't know what she wants or what you want. But if you care about her, don't give up so easily. Sometimes it takes a little time for people to figure out their hearts."

Wyatt sighed, running a hand through his hair. "Yeah, well, time isn't exactly on my side, is it? With Everett around, I might be out of the running before I even had a chance."

Clara shook her head, a spark of determination in her eyes. "Not if I have anything to say about it, Wyatt. Just... trust me, okay? And maybe try being a little more honest with Sadie about how you feel."

Wyatt glanced at her, a flicker of hope lighting in his eyes. "You think I've still got a chance?"

Clara smirked, leaning back in her seat. "Oh, I *know* you do. Now, drink your coffee and get ready, because things are about to get interesting."

As the lights of Magnolia Springs began to twinkle against in the night, Miss Pearl's plan was already in motion. Everett, Sadie, Wyatt, and even Clara had become unwitting players in a carefully orchestrated dance of emotions, each step drawing them closer to the connections that would change their lives.

And as Miss Pearl sat by her window, watching her town, she allowed herself a small, satisfied smile. "Well, Magnolia Springs," she murmured, "let's see if we can't bring a little more love into this town before winter's end."

Milton Keynes UK
Ingram Content Group UK Ltd.
UKHW021121111124
451035UK00016B/1143